GAMES FOR READING

GAMES FOR READING

PLAYFUL WAYS TO HELP YOUR CHILD READ

WRITTEN BY **Peggy Kaye**

WITH ILLUSTRATIONS
BY THE AUTHOR

PANTHEON BOOKS
NEW YORK

All rights reserved under International and Pan-American
Copyright Conventions. Published in the United States
by Pantheon Books, a division of Random House, Inc.,
New York, and simultaneously in Canada by Random
House of Canada Limited, Toronto.

Grateful acknowledgment is made to the publisher,
Vanguard Press, Inc., for permission to reprint a poem
from *And to Think That I Saw It on Mulberry Street* by
Dr. Seuss. Copyright 1937 by "Dr. Seuss" (Theodore
Seuss Geisel). Copyright renewed 1964 by "Dr. Seuss"
(Theodore Seuss Geisel).

Library of Congress Cataloging in Publication Data
Kaye, Peggy, 1948–
    Games for reading.

    Bibliography: p.
    1. Children—Books and reading.   2. Reading games.
I. Title.
Z1037.K26   1984   649'.58   83–19403
ISBN 0–394–52785–2
ISBN 0–394–72149–7 (pbk.)

Manufactured in the United States of America

First Edition

Book design by Naomi Osnos

CONTENTS

ACKNOWLEDGMENTS

I owe more than I can say to the students and teachers of a school on the East Side of Manhattan called the Learning Community. The Learning Community was tiny—it never had more than seventy children at a time—but it was full of ideals and warmth, and was just the place to develop games to help children learn. Unfortunately the school went the way of too many tiny institutions in our big society, and folded. But I like to think that a bit of the Learning Community survives in the pages of *Games for Reading*. The book tells many stories about children from that school. I have changed names and drawn some composite portraits, but I'm sure the old alumni will still recognize themselves.

Mary Katherine Barker was one of the Learning Community teachers and actually invented some of the games. She read the manuscript and offered excellent criticisms, as did Nancy Garrity, Elizabeth Kaye, Wilhemina Kraber, and Katherine O'Donnell. The judgment and good taste of my editor, Sara Bershtel, improved the book enormously. Thank you also to Helena Franklin and Amy Johnson.

Paul Berman played a major role in getting *Games for Reading* written. He took time from his own writing to give me help and guidance. He clarified my ideas. He straightened out sentences and paragraphs. His intelligence and writing talent enrich every page of the book, and to him the book is dedicated.

INTRODUCTION

For several years, I was the reading teacher at a small private elementary school. I taught children with every kind of problem—children who were hyperactive, undermotivated, or confused. Some of my pupils spoke Spanish or Korean better than English. Others had no problems at all; some, in fact, were too advanced for their regular classes and were coming to me for extra work. With all these children. I used the methods every reading teacher uses—I taught formal lessons, I gave assignments in workbooks, I listened while children read aloud. But I also used games. We played dozens of games in my workroom—games with rhymes or tall tales, games with pencil and paper, games with playing boards and tokens or scissors and paste, games that got me and my students hopping around the room and tacking up funny things on the walls. *Games for Reading* shares these games with you.

Games have three great virtues. First, you can use them to teach nearly every skill a beginning reader needs to learn. If a first-grader has trouble telling *b* from *d*, games can improve his eye for tiny details. If a second-grader is working on remembering words, games can help train his memory. The right game can zero in on any need or interest a child might have.

These games are fun—that's their second virtue. They draw on the one skill all children have in abundance, the ability to play. When children play, their resistance to learning goes down and their willingness to apply themselves goes up. They never absorb ideas more easily than when they're having a good time. And they're happy to play these games over and over again, which is useful in acquiring certain skills. Games take the drudgery out of drill.

Finally, the games get parents more involved in their children's education. I realize that many parents are shy about teaching their children and feel that teaching should be left to teachers. In general, I agree; but parents do teach their children in many areas every day—perhaps without realizing it. They teach children to throw a football, cross a street, make a bed or a sandwich; they help with homework, and there's even a method of violin instruction that has parents practice along with their children. Why shouldn't they help with reading, too—in a fashion that doesn't interfere with school?

Games are the perfect way for parents to give reading help without turning into mean taskmasters. In fact, the games can be as much fun for adults as for children. And while some require time and energy on the parent's part, most do not. There are valuable reading games that can be played in five minutes while straightening the house or waiting for the bus. There are useful games that adults can enjoy with children while watching TV. Most of the mothers and fathers I meet work full time and are extremely busy. These games fit into even their hectic schedules.

Games for Reading offers seventy-six games, all of them tried and true. They train beginning readers (meaning first-through-third-graders, by and large) in virtually every skill required for reading. Playing these games is extremely beneficial for children who are stumbling at their studies; the games offer alternative ways of tackling areas of difficulty. But they are equally valuable for children who find reading a breeze. Children who have trouble playing baseball may require special sessions devoted to batting and fielding; but even the greatest athlete can benefit from a game of catch. Just so with good students and these reading games.

Exactly what skills are needed for reading? Let me describe them by pointing to a child who learned to read effortlessly by herself. When Sara entered first grade, she already knew the alphabet and many of the sounds letters make, and she could read a few words. By the end of that year, she was quite a fluent reader. Sara really didn't need teaching at all—but not because of any mysterious talent. It was just that she instinctively grasped the main approaches to reading.

I watched Sara at work in her reading group one day. She was reading aloud and doing fine, when up came a word she didn't know. The sentence with the unknown word read like this:

Carl ran ——————— down the street.

How to decipher the unknown word? Sara saw that *qu* were the first letters in the word. Knowing her letter sounds, she understood that the word began with the sound *kw*. She also grasped the general drift of the sentence. Putting together these bits of knowledge —the initial sound of the word and the general meaning of the sentence—she tried to fill in the blank with a reasonable guess. *Quickly* was a good guess. *Carl ran QUICKLY down the street.* It was that or *quietly*. Does anyone run quietly? Or perhaps *quacking*. Would Carl quack? No, *quickly* was the word.

Two pages later, *quickly* reappeared. This time she read it without hesitation; having figured out the mystery word earlier, she remembered it now. Thus Sara taught herself a new word with no help from the teacher.

She didn't know it, of course, but Sara had made use of the three major methods of reading instruction. First, she had a firm idea of the relation between letters and sounds. The *qu* told her exactly how the beginning of the word would sound. She could also listen to this beginning sound and imagine other sounds blending with it to make a whole word. These skills constitute the sounding-out (or phonics) approach to reading.

Next, she had an instinct for meaning, an idea of sentence structure, and a good vocabulary. This helped her make a logical guess in order to complete the sentence. Attention to the meaning of stories, awareness of the structure of sentences, and familiarity with many words add up to skill in reading comprehension—the ability to understand. That's the second main approach to reading.

Sara also remembered the word and knew it the next time it appeared. *Quickly* became one of the words she knew at first sight. Memorizing words so that you can recognize them at once is the sight-vocabulary approach to reading.

Sara's great strength was the ability to take these three approaches—sounding out, reading comprehension, and sight vocabulary—and work them together in a single effort of mind. Many children have a hard time doing this; indeed, learning to combine these skills is one of the greatest intellectual tasks a child will ever perform. But Sara had an advantage that made the job easier: she loved to read. She liked everything about reading—the books, the pictures, the words, the stories. Reading was a wonderful part of life to her, like playing with dolls; figuring out the hard parts of reading a story was no more onerous to her than putting the clothes on a doll and pulling them off again. Love of reading made it easy for her to focus her full attention on the printed page.

The games I describe are designed to lead any child, with a parent's help, along the path unusual children like Sara follow on their own. The games stick precisely to the three major areas of reading instruction.

Part One offers games to improve sight vocabulary. Some of these games give children practice at memorizing, which is an important part of expanding sight vocabulary. Others train the eye, which is equally important. To develop a sight vocabulary, children must be able to look at words very closely and make subtle distinctions. They must be able to tell that words that look quite similar—*went* and *want*, for example—are actually different; and they must see that certain words that look quite different—for instance, *orange* and **orange**—are really the same. The games in Part One focus on skills like these. There are also games to drill children on specific words that come up often and so demand quick recognition.

Part Two offers games that develop skills for sounding out. To sound out words, children must learn to hear in precise detail. They must distinguish between similar sounds, like the *b*-sound and the *p*-sound. They must then blend different sounds together into a single word, such as the *m*-sound, the *a*-as-in-*cat*-sound, and the *t*-sound that make *mat.* They must relate sounds to individual letters and groups of letters, and be able to do all this accurately and instantly. The games in this section train children in exactly these skills.

Part Three is for reading comprehension. These games strengthen children's ability to learn new words, to reason logically when using words, and to sharpen their instinct for sentence structure. Reading comprehension also requires skills that are less technical—the capacity to think imaginatively, for instance. How can you read and understand a fairy tale if your imagination doesn't prompt you to enter into the story? Some children need a little help in freeing their imagination, and this, too, figures in the section on reading comprehension.

All three of these sections should help strengthen children's interest in reading, but Part Four is designed specifically for this purpose. It offers games to make reading fun, to get children to love books, to want to read.

There's no set method for using *Games for Reading.* Some parents may play favorite games regularly. Other mothers and fathers will keep the book on a shelf until a rainy Saturday, then pull it out and play two or three games, just as something to do. Certain parents have the time and desire to prepare the game boards and special playing cards that some games require, and are happy to spend lots of energy over such games. Others will stick to games that require no preparation and can be enjoyed during car rides or while cooking supper. Whatever pattern fits your family is fine. And it's not at all necessary to go through this book from beginning to end. You may start with Part One, but you can just as well begin with any of the other three. Feel free to move back and forth from one section to the next. As long as you pick out games that are fun for you and fun for your child, you've made the right choices.

Your child is likely to find one or another section harder than the others, depending on his special areas of strength and weakness. I had one student, Helena, who had no trouble sounding out words, but slowed down when it came to memorizing them. It didn't surprise me that she found Part Two (sounding-out games) easy, and Part One (sight-vocabulary games, which includes memory games) difficult. What to do with a child like this? Play both the hard games and the easy ones. The hard games work on a child's weaknesses; the easy games build on strengths. That's the best way to help any beginning reader.

Occasionally I've indicated that a game shouldn't be played until a child reaches second or third grade. Even if a child is doing advanced work in first grade, it's still better to hold off on these particular games, in order to avoid possible conflict between the games' methods and the specific techniques that your child's teacher prefers for introducing new skills. But never worry that a child is too old for any game that he enjoys. Professional musicians practice scales, and children in the first three or four grades can benefit from even the simplest games. When a child has serious learning problems, games, although helpful, don't constitute a cure-all. Children with serious problems need help from trained professionals. If your child is already receiving special help, you might ask his tutor or teacher to pick out appropriate games for you to play at home.

There's one important rule that applies to every part of this book. You must always remember how important you are to your child and how much he or she wants to impress you. Because of this, your child may find it painful to fail in front of you. Your attitude toward mistakes, therefore, becomes crucial to the success of these games. If mistakes are fine with you, your child will have an easier time playing. You can help by being nice about your child's errors—for instance, by saying: "Oops, a mistake.

Don't worry, I make mistakes, too." Or: "It's OK to give the wrong answer. If you always knew the right answers, this game wouldn't be fun any more."

And having fun is the key thing. If these games aren't fun, they aren't working. With each game, ask yourself if you and your child are having a good time. If the answer is no, try another game; there are lots of them. Or you may want to tinker with a set of rules to suit yourselves, or invent new games based on the ones here. Sometimes it's worth trying a game again; your child may dislike a certain game today, yet love it tomorrow—or next year— and you may feel the same way. Some of the games call on you to do silly things or jump around the room. Tonight you may not feel up to that. But come Saturday morning, jumping around and acting silly may seem like a great idea—especially when you know it's helping your child learn to read.

GAMES FOR READING

PART ONE

Games for
Learning Words

chapter 1.

Words Everywhere

Jacob, an eager first-grader, came marching into my workroom the first day of school, looked me in the eye, and blurted out, "I want to read." Who could resist such a request? I walked to the chalkboard and wrote SCHOOL in big letters. I asked Jacob to name each letter: "s-c-h-o-o-l." He knew the alphabet and could say every one. Then I told him to trace the letters with his finger. Slowly, carefully, Jacob put out his hand and began to trace. "That's a word," I said. "The word is *school*." Jacob smiled. "School," he repeated. "Hey, Jacob, you just read that word. Can you read it again?" "School!" he boomed. "Terrific! Come back tomorrow and I'll help you read some more words."

Jacob did come back—the next day and the next week and the next month. Sometimes he came on his own, sometimes with a reading group. He worked hard, and by the end of the school year he was reading away.

Much of the time was spent introducing Jacob to new reading words. I tried to make learning these words as exciting as learning *school* had been on his very first day. That is the goal of the games in this chapter: to generate excitement about learning to read, and to keep that excitement alive. Some of the games spotlight individual words. Your child will color in words, skip on them, and hunt for them in supermarkets. Some games make use of labels. In one game you'll put word labels up all over the house; in another you'll label photographs; in still another, you'll label your own body. Your child will probably memorize many words while playing these games, and that's fine. But it's also OK if he or she doesn't remember a single word. Memorization is important for reading; it's one of the objects of these games. But not the main one. Excitement—enthusiasm for reading—is the main object.

Browse through the chapter, pick out the games that seem fun to play, and try them out. If you have fun with a game, your child will begin to associate reading with enjoyment. Nothing could be more valuable. And if some memorization takes place, too, all the better.

GIFT WORDS

MATERIALS

index cards

pen

gift-wrapping paper

Here is a very simple game, one of the simplest in this book. Think of a word that has special significance for your child. *Baseball, gymnastics, balloon, hamster, computer,* or *pizza* are likely candidates. With a little work, you can give this special, significant word to your child as a gift. Get an index card and write the word down. If you're in the mood and have the time, decorate the card.

Take gift-wrapping paper—colored tissue paper is nice—and wrap the card. Ribbons or stickers to decorate the wrapping would be nicer still.

Pick an appropriate time of day—dinnertime, after school, or early in the morning—and give your child his gift word. If your child can't read the word, read it for him. Now the word is his. He may carry it around with him all day. He may save it in a treasured box. He may lose it within five minutes. Whatever happens should be all right with you. Some children don't particularly enjoy or value gift words. If that's true of your child, look in this book for a different activity. Other children unreservedly love these words. They feel pride and delight every time they receive one, and are eager to read them. If your child reacts enthusiastically to receiving his first gift word, then give him more. You might give a gift word a week, or every other week. As long as these words are fun to give and fun to receive, keep them coming.

I remember one day when I gave a word to Blanche. She stomped into her class, held the card above her head, and shouted, "Look at the present Peggy gave me! It says *birthday.*" Well, that was it. I had to sit right down and make word presents for the entire class.

POSTER WORDS

MATERIALS

large piece of paper,
poster board, or oak tag
(at least 11″ x 14″)
coloring materials like
colored markers, crayons,
colored pencils, or
watercolor paints
stick-on stars and sparkles

*T*here are posters for TV stars and posters for movie stars—why not posters for word stars? A word star is easy to define. If a word is especially interesting to your child, it's a star. The kinds of words appropriate for GIFT WORDS are appropriate here as well. Sports words like *hockey, basketball,* or *bowling.* Flower words like *rose, tulip,* or *iris.* Food words: *popcorn, ice cream,* or *grapes.* Or monster words: *witch, werewolf, mummy,* or *ghost.* Whatever the word, write it on a piece of paper, oak tag, or poster board that is at least 11″ x 14″. The paper can be larger—14″ x 17″, 18″ x 22″, 30″ x 40″. The bigger the paper, the more impressive the poster. The letters should be the open type that are usually perfected by seventh-graders:

TULIP   WITCH

Now the fun starts. You and your child collect a pile of coloring materials—paints, crayons, stars, and sparkles—and go to town. Make the word light up Broadway.

Hang this poster in a place of honor.

When your child gets bored with one poster, create another. You might make multiword posters: for instance, a zoo animal poster, a musical instrument poster, a body word poster.

An entire wall covered with word posters would certainly be a conversation starter.

3-D WORDS

MATERIALS

play dough
cardboard
glue
paint brush
tempera paint

*I*t was hard to get Larry to concentrate on reading, or on anything else. He was a perpetual motion machine and his mind was as jittery as his body. The only time I saw Larry work with concentrated attention was when he modeled little clay figures.

So I started using play dough to focus his attention on reading. We began making letters and words out of play dough. This was a turning point for Larry. He couldn't learn, at this stage of his life, by studying with paper and pencil; but he could learn by studying with big wads of play dough.

We started with a four-color play dough kit. At first Larry wanted to make cars and little animals. I told him that cars could wait and that now we'd make words. According to the rules I laid down, he could make any word at all. Larry chose *baseball* and immediately we got to work. We rolled the play dough into pencil-thick coils. Eventually we had enough coils and began forming letters. I showed Larry how to pinch the letters together to make firm joints.

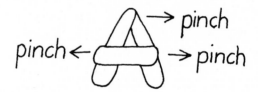

The letters were in four colors. Some letters were capitals, some weren't, and they were every which size. Even so, they made a beautiful word:

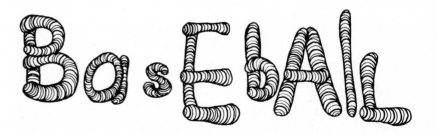

After *baseball* was complete, he was ready for the next word —*Yankees*. We rolled the appropriate coils. When *Yankees* was finished, he wanted to make his own name, *Larry*. At this point our work time was over. I told Larry he could save one word, but the others would have to be mushed up. Larry decided to mush up his own name and *baseball*. He put the red letters back with the red play dough, and the blue letters back with the blue play dough, and I gave him separate containers for mixed colors.

We left *Yankees* out to dry. The drying took a day or two. The letters needed to be flipped over during this time in order to dry all the way through. Unfortunately the *Y* in *Yankees* split in two, which upset Larry quite a bit. Not to worry: we waited until the broken parts were completely dry, then I took a good brand of white glue and cemented the pieces together.

The letters were now intact, but they were still separate letters. Instead of leaving them that way, we made a 3-D word plaque. I cut a piece of cardboard to a suitable size. Larry painted the cardboard with orange tempera paint. When the paint was dry, we glued the letters onto the cardboard. Larry was terrifically proud of this plaque. He kept it on display in his bedroom.

Making play dough words and plaques appealed to Larry. We started making them on a regular basis. Larry was really a sport about it, so I decided to be one, too. After he made a couple of words, I always let him make a boat or a rabbit.

JUMBO WORDS

MATERIALS

colored chalk

Nathaniel Hawthorne once described going to the beach and writing his name in gigantic letters in the sand. Each letter was so huge it took two or three strides to get across. Hawthorne said this was child's play. He was right; and a most useful kind of play, too.

Here is a variation of Hawthorne's beach game. It works perfectly well on pavement or blacktop, or indoors on linoleum or wood floors. Wherever you play, except at the beach, you'll need a piece of chalk. (On linoleum or wood, you'll have to press the chalk good and hard. Don't worry—it comes off easily.) Your child says a word, and you do the writing. Your child might say his name, or might name a sports hero, a food, a monster, a favorite animal. Anything will do, really. Let's say he picks *lion*. Then you write *lion* in great big jumbo letters. Now tell your child to stride along the route of the letters. When he's finished striding, tell him to hop, jump, skip, spin, crawl, tiptoe, baby-step, giant-step, walk backwards, and boog-a-loo.

Maybe you can think of more ways to move. Good—try them out. After this physical workout, *lion* will be a wee bit harder for any child to forget. When your child is fed up with one word, wipe it off and write a new one. Or move to a new spot on the pavement.

By the way, your child may want you to stride, hop, jump, skip, and so forth across the letters, too. So why not do it? I jump around the letters myself, although I feel a little foolish. It was good enough for Hawthorne, I figure.

*T*he educator Sylvia Ashton-Warner, teaching Maori children in New Zealand to read, came up with a very clever idea. She looked for "key" words—words that have vivid emotional meanings for children. Every day she elicited one key word from each child in her class and wrote them down on large sheets. The sheets said: "alligators," "war dance," "wild pig," "ghost," "Daddy"—words like that. Ashton-Warner's theory was that Maori children would learn these words with a single long look. This actually worked, she found. The words were so interesting the children had no trouble learning them.

I duplicated this experiment with my own students. My children weren't Maoris from New Zealand but students in a private school on the Upper East Side of Manhattan. Their "key" words were sometimes the same as the Maori children's and sometimes a little different—words like "video," "teddy bear," "mugger," and "doughnut." Just like Sylvia Ashton-Warner, I wrote these down on large sheets. The children on the Upper East Side turned out to be a little slower than the Maoris of New Zealand. One long look was not enough for my children to learn the words. They needed several looks, often many looks. But in general, Ashton-Warner's idea proved to be an excellent one. The children did have an easier time learning "key" words than the boring old words that early vocabularies are conventionally made of. They learned words like *kiss* or *hurricane* quicker than they learned words like *look* or *into*. It worked in New Zealand; it worked in Manhattan; it might work at your house.

Here's how to proceed, not with a whole classroom, but with one or several children of your own. Get a file box and a bunch of index cards. You might wrap the box and give it to your child as a gift. Explain that the box is going to hold a collection of words, words just for him or her. Let your child select the word. Tell him that he can add one and only one word a day to the box. Every day (or as often as possible) sit together and decide what word that will be. Urge your child to think hard about his word. Occasionally children will pop out with amazing ideas. But more often children's first word ideas are pretty bland. Some blandness in the box is OK, but a boxful of boring words is not. You will probably have to stimulate interesting words by talking about interesting things. The right topic of conversation will produce colorful words. Maybe your child got into a fight with a bitter enemy. In that case, words like *liar, cheater, creep*, or *rotten* might take on special significance. Talking about a predicted snowstorm might generate words like *blizzard, freezing, snowman*, or *Eskimo.* You and your child could get into a discussion of scary places. Then words like *cemetery, jail, haunted house, ghost*, or *volcano* might be powerful additions to a word box. Even talking about TV can be fruitful. For some children, *Cookie Monster* may actually be a one-look word.

After your child decides on a word, write it on an index card. If your child wants to write the word for himself, let him, even if his handwriting is very messy. Then put the card in the collection box. Whenever you have a little extra time, take the cards out and let your child read as many as he can. Help him read the rest.

An extra benefit of this game is to generate an interest in unusual vocabulary that you and your child can share and that can last long after the child has progressed beyond elementary stages of reading. "I saw an interesting word this morning," you might find yourselves saying to one another some day. "Syzygy—it's something that happens in outer space. . . ."

You start with words like *kiss* and *ghost*—and who knows where it will lead?

*T*he case of Ralph, a superactive first-grader: why weren't his reading skills developing? He couldn't seem to learn letter sounds, couldn't memorize words. I tested him, and he didn't have any learning disabilities. He simply needed lots of drill. But drill was the one thing he couldn't stomach; he was too active. His mind wandered. Worse, his body wandered.

What Ralph needed was a superactive wandering game that incidentally offered lots of drill in memorizing words. WORD HUNT was the game. Here's how it worked. Ralph and I talked about supermarkets. We tried to think of words that can be found in supermarkets, words like *tomato, orange, chocolate, corn, large, jumbo.* I asked him to choose two of these words. He came up with *chocolate* (naturally) and *orange.*

I wrote the words on a sheet of paper designed as a scorecard:

chocolate	orange
Total	Total

Since we were going to write on the scorecard, I taped it to a book to give it a hard backing.

Then it was off to the supermarket. "Ralph," I said as we walked to the store, "we're going to wander all over the aisles. We're going to hunt for these two words and see which one you can find the most times. It is a contest between *chocolate* and *orange.* We'll see which one wins the word-hunt game." Ralph was already running down the aisle. I called him back to discuss the rules of the game.

MATERIALS

paper
pencil
a book
optional: index cards

I told him he had five minutes to hunt for the word *chocolate*. He would get one point each time he saw the word. But each time it had to be a new product. He couldn't get twenty points for twenty packages of M&M's. He could go to any section of the store he wanted, but he couldn't run or shout. Points would be taken from him if he ran through the aisles. He had to show me the places he saw *chocolate* before he could score. If he showed me *chocolate* written on a package and I agreed it was worth a point, he got to write a mark on his scorecard. This helped ensure calmer behavior; he couldn't score a point unless he checked with me, and I wasn't running around the market.

After five minutes, we would switch words. He would start to hunt for *orange* (plurals were allowed, so that a sign saying "oranges 59¢/lb." was worth a point). He'd have a five-minute hunt for *orange*; then we'd add up the number of points he had scored for each word. We'd see if *chocolate* or *orange* won.

Ralph stalked the aisles, full of excitement and enthusiasm. But it was soon clear that he needed help discovering the words. I showed him a box and asked him if he could find *chocolate* printed on it. He had to locate the word on the package and point it out to me. This wasn't always easy. Words come in different typefaces, and Ralph had to figure out the difference between type-

faces and letters. It was hard work for him to concentrate on the words when he was all fired up. Nevertheless, we played the game. Ralph found a lot of *chocolates*. After five minutes, we switched to *orange.* He found a lot of *oranges.* Ten minutes was the enjoyment limit for this game.

chocolate	orange
IIII IIIII III	III IIII II
Total 12	Total 9

Over the weeks, as we hunted for various words, Ralph needed less help. He could wander the aisles pointing out hunt words left and right. Eventually he needed no help at all. He began to memorize words, and thrilled both of us by remembering *orange* even on a day when we were hunting for *milk.*

We didn't always hunt in the supermarket. Occasionally we'd take a neighborhood stroll. I gave Ralph four 3" x 5" index cards. Each card had a word or phrase written on it that could be found on signs in the immediate area—words and phrases like *bank, flowers, dry cleaner, bus stop.* During a fifteen-minute walk, Ralph had to find the words or phrases from all four cards. When he found the fourth word or phrase, he won. Watching him eagerly scrutinize each sign we passed was a teacher's treat. Ralph was deeply involved in learning to read. He'd begun to discover how exciting reading can be.

For you as a parent, it only involves a few extra minutes during a shopping trip or while doing neighborhood errands to write down some hunt words. But be warned, beginning to read is like beginning to talk. Once your child realizes he can read the signs in his neighborhood or labels in the supermarket, he may not stop. "Look, Peggy, that says *bank*, and that says *flowers*, and that says *red*, and that says *milk*, and that says *clothes*, and that says *ice cream*, and that says . . . "

CHARADE CARDS

MATERIALS

index cards or pieces of paper

pen or pencil

storage box

*T*his game needs at least three players, although it can be played with more. At least one player must be a reader of great expertise: for instance, you.

Debbie was a first-grader who resented leaving her class and coming to see me, the reading teacher. She regarded school as a social event that was too frequently interrupted by work. Naturally, she wasn't doing very well. One morning, watching Debbie in her classroom, I noticed that she was the class performer. When the class was talking about plants, Debbie jumped up and acted out a flower swaying in the breeze. When they were discussing sports, Debbie was busy swinging an imaginary bat and running nonexistent bases. She was disruptive, but she was also creative and clever. I wondered if I could use her love of hamming to help her read.

We started to play CHARADE CARDS. We needed another player for this game, so I asked Debbie to bring a friend along, and she came with Ralph. In my hand I held ten index cards. Each card had an animal word written on it: *cat, dog, lion, rabbit, bird, snake, mouse, monkey, goat,* and *horse.* I told Debbie to pick a card. The card she took said *snake.* She didn't read *snake* out loud. Instead she came over and whispered it in my ear. I nodded my head, confirming that she'd read the word correctly. My nod was also the signal for Debbie to become a snake. She slipped to the floor and squiggled and squirmed. She flicked her tongue. She was a very convincing snake. No doubt Ralph knew Debbie was a snake before she finished her routine. But we had a rule that no guesses were allowed until the act was complete. After Debbie had her turn, Ralph said, "snake," then picked his own card. The children took turns reading, acting, and guessing. Some animal cards got picked twice. We had two elephants and two cats that first charade day. When we finished working. I put the cards in a box, ready for another time.

Next time came and Debbie showed no signs of resentment. She picked a new friend and away we went. I told Debbie that today there were nonanimal cards added to the deck. These cards said *skating, bowling, hammer, saw, mirror,* and *flowers.* We played as before, and Debbie gave bravura performances in both acting and reading.

If you have more than one child in your family, get them all into the act. A beginning reader gains reading practice with CHARADE CARDS, but both younger and older children like to play (you'll have to read the cards for nonreaders).

Here is a list of charade words and phrases:

basketball	writing a letter
baseball	icing a cake
soccer	playing the violin
swimming	sun
riding a bike	rain
sweeping the floor	monster
brushing your teeth	chair
making breakfast	sleep
eating soup	throw
sharpening a pencil	open a can
reading a book	feeling sick

. . . plus the animals of your choice. Write some of these down on index cards and you're all set.

PICTURE LABELS

MATERIALS

photographs
(these can be from magazines, calendars, the family snapshot album or any other source)

paper

pen

transparent tape

*L*ynn was an exceptionally meticulous child whose disciplined nature showed in everything she did. Her cubby was neat, her desk clean, her papers well organized, her handwriting clear and legible. That's why I knew she'd like PICTURE LABELS. Although sloppy children enjoy this game, its organized and precise quality is especially appealing to neatniks like Lynn.

The game started with Lynn picking out a picture from my collection of photographs. She chose a magazine ad showing an elegantly dressed gentleman relaxing in the country air. We started talking about this picture. I asked her to name everything she saw in it. She listed the obvious things first: *man, sweater, jacket, pants, shirt, tie, fence.* Once she'd stated the obvious, I pushed her to see details. I asked questions like, "What do you call this?" "What's the name of that?" "What color is this?" Occasionally I taught her the meaning of a new word—for instance, *lapel.* As a result of these questions her list of picture words grew longer and longer: *eyes, nose, hair, hand, skin, mouth, ear, green, blue, tan, neck, button, pocket, sleeve, collar, lapel, cane, grass, lawn, wrinkle.* Each time she said a word she wrote it on a small slip of paper. When she needed spelling help, I provided it. (Your child's handwriting might not be up to this task. If it is not, write the labels for him.) After the labels were written, our next job was taping them to the photograph. Lynn read each label before she taped it in place. It wasn't long before the whole photograph was covered with labels.

I'm not sure why taping labels all over a photograph feels so satisfying. But it does; something about the power of words to correspond with reality, I'm sure. In any case, as soon as we finished labeling one picture, Lynn reached for another, ready to label all over again.

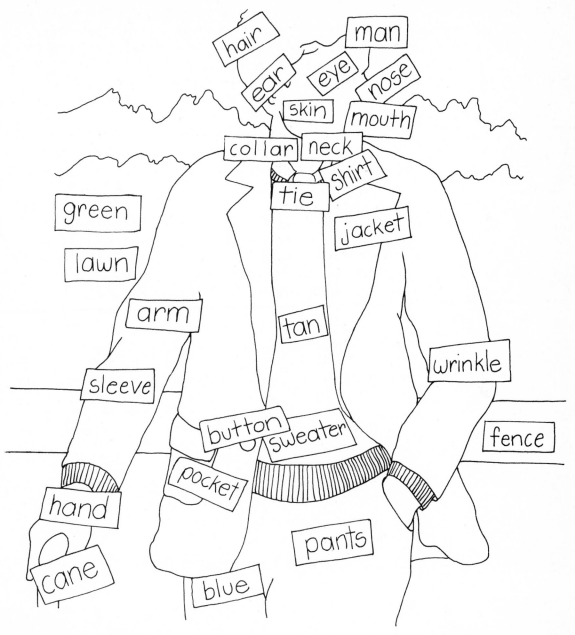

LABEL THE HOUSE

MATERIALS

masking tape
transparent tape
index cards
colored markers

*L*ABEL THE HOUSE is PICTURE LABELS on a grand scale. You tape name tags on objects in your home. These labels teach your child all sorts of new words.

Start in the kitchen (or any room you want). Sit with your child and start thinking of kitchen words. When one of you thinks of a word, take an index card and write it down. Then tape the label to the appropriate place. You might put a *cup* label on a cup, a *cabinet* label on a cabinet, a *table* label on the table, and so on. For long words such as *refrigerator*, tape together a couple of cards to make the letters big enough. With short words and little objects, cut the index card down. For faraway objects like a high cabinet, write in large letters, perhaps using a couple of cards.

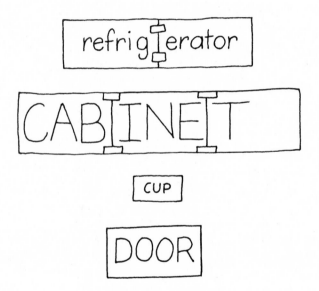

Usually it's easier if you make the labels yourself. Of course, if your child is eager to write a label, that's fine. He or she may need help with spelling, but that's OK. Not all of this labeling needs to be done in a single day. You can tape a few words now and a few words later, until your kitchen looks like this:

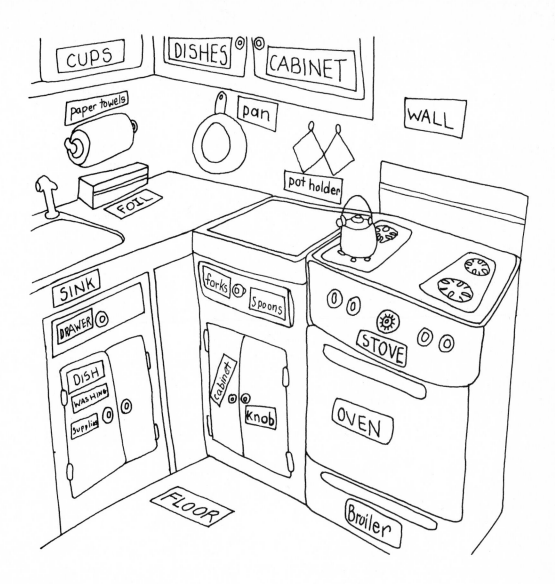

Your kitchen has now become a word room.

Initially your child will take great interest in the cards, but this may fade in a few days. To keep a child's attention on the words, you might try this spelling game. When you and your child are sitting in the kitchen surrounded by labels, ask him to spell label words—for instance, *stove, dish, cup, door*, or even long words like *linoleum*. To spell, he'll have to look carefully at the labels. Even if he wrote every label himself, he might not remember how the words are spelled. By examining these labels carefully, he'll be studying the words. If you have an older child at home, he can play, too. The older child closes his eyes and spells the words. The younger child checks his sibling's spelling by comparing it with the labels. Remember that, with an early reader, the purpose of this game is not so much to help him spell, but to help him remember the word well enough to read it. Even a few minutes of this game while snacking or doing dinner dishes will work.

When you've had it with kitchen words, start labeling other rooms. As you label the house, your child will learn words like *sofa, carpet, picture, rug, lamp, magazine, bathroom, tub, closet, bed, light switch, doorknob, television, pillow*, and *radiator*. Labels all over the house may disrupt your decorating scheme, but think of the rewards. Your home looks strange; your child's vocabulary expands.

Eventually you'll take down the cards. But the labels in your child's room can be more permanent. Labels on the toy box, bookshelf, and dresser drawers might actually prove practical. Once a child can read all the labels, he can no longer claim, when you ask him to straighten up, "I didn't know where to put it." He'll need a new excuse for his messy room.

BODY WORDS

Susan was a kidder, prankster, and giggler, and she invented this game. One day I decided to teach her how to read words naming parts of the body. I made little word cards from slips of paper, saying *nose, hand, face, finger, eye*, and *mouth*. My plan was to tape the words to the wall and try to help Susan memorize them. But Susan had another idea. She sashayed into my workroom and spotted the cards with the tape already on them. She grabbed one of the cards and announced, "I know what this says; this says *nose.*" Then, amid a flutter of giggles, she taped the card to the tip of my nose.

"Very funny," I said. "You know what this says? This says *ear.*" I taped the card right on her earlobe. Now we were both giggling. We started taking turns reading words and taping cards on appropriate body parts. When Susan had trouble reading a word, I helped her. Once all the words were taped, we took the cards off. Then we started reading and taping again. We found that a certain leeway in placing the cards was necessary. The *face* card was placed on a forehead or a chin. The *mouth* card didn't tape the mouth shut. The *eye* card wasn't actually blocking an eye. We also found that it's bad to tape the cards too firmly; it hurts when you pull them off.

There are so many different possibilities, you and your child could find yourselves completely covered with paper slips. Here is a list of some body words.

face	back	thigh
hand	backside	knee
eye	hip	foot
eyebrow	waist	heel
forehead	arm	hair
nose	hand	nail
chin	finger	lip
mouth	skin	neck

The first time you play, pick out five or ten words. You can add others next time. If you giggle a lot the first time, there's sure to be a next time.

MATERIALS
paper
pen
transparent tape

chapter 2.

Games for the Eye

When Nicole began first grade, nothing excited her more than learning to read. She swelled with pride at every new word she learned. Unfortunately, things began to change after a while. Nicole was no longer able to keep up with her reading group. As she fell behind, her excitement turned to anxiety, her pride to self-doubt. She started to feel stupid.

What changed Nicole's success into failure? In her first reading books, words were introduced slowly and repetitively. This was perfect for her. She could remember words taught at a slow pace. After a few months, however, the pace sped up: new words were introduced one after another and were repeated less frequently. Nicole was expected to increase her rate of learning words. But she couldn't.

Several problems interfered with Nicole's progress. First, she had a hard time remembering words. She might see a word—for instance, *house*—a dozen times a day, but the thirteenth time she still couldn't remember it. Second, she confused similar-looking letters like *b* and *d.* This resulted in her reading *big* instead of *dig,* and *nob* instead of *nod.* Third, she confused similar-looking words, such as *went* and *want.* She also reshuffled letters. She read *was* instead of *saw,* and *left* instead of *felt.*

All of these separate difficulties have something in common. They are problems in visual perception. The more problems a child has in this area, the harder it is for him to learn how to read. Imagine learning to read *dog* if sometimes it appears to you as *bog,* other times as *pog,* and occasionally as *gog.* You'd have a hard time.

There is no such thing as perfect perceptual vision. All children have difficulties, at least sometimes. At best, a child will confuse an occasional *b* and *d,* or perhaps have sporadic problems memorizing words. At worst, a child's visual world will be so askew that he can't begin reading without help from a trained specialist.

Nicole's problems, although more severe than most children's, were still fairly manageable. Games in Nicole's case proved exceptionally useful. We didn't use word games, but puzzles, mazes, and drawings instead. These games served three purposes: they sharpened her visual perception, trained her visual memory, and gave her practice recognizing individual letters. I use these games with all beginning readers. Most don't need as much help as Nicole, but every child can benefit. You'll find these games useful even with good readers.

MAZES

*T*he world can be divided into two camps: those who love solving mazes and those who don't. I myself am a maze lover. Therefore I was delighted to discover that solving mazes is a terrific eye exercise. Consider the visual concentration that goes into solving a maze. Merely to keep within the maze trails takes visual skill. Maze solvers scan the trails, looking for the right path. Their eyes scout along an intricate route, branch off to a second route, experiment with a third. All of this constitutes an exercise in close visual perception—exactly the kind of exercise children need in tracing the shapes of letters and words, and to train their eyes to follow a line of print. Of course, I don't tell children that mazes are useful for reading. Why spoil the fun? The educational value of a good maze is my private business.

There are surprisingly few commercially available mazes for beginners. That's why I started drawing them myself. On the following pages are several of my homemade mazes. You can photocopy them, or let your child work right in the book. I hope that these mazes will inspire you to try drawing your own. Maze-drawing doesn't require much concentration: you can draw mazes and watch Sunday afternoon football simultaneously. And mazes don't require artistic ability. If you can draw a crooked line, you can draw a maze.

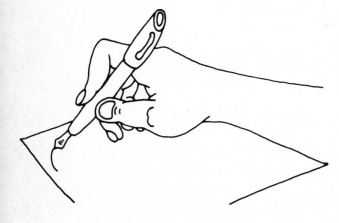

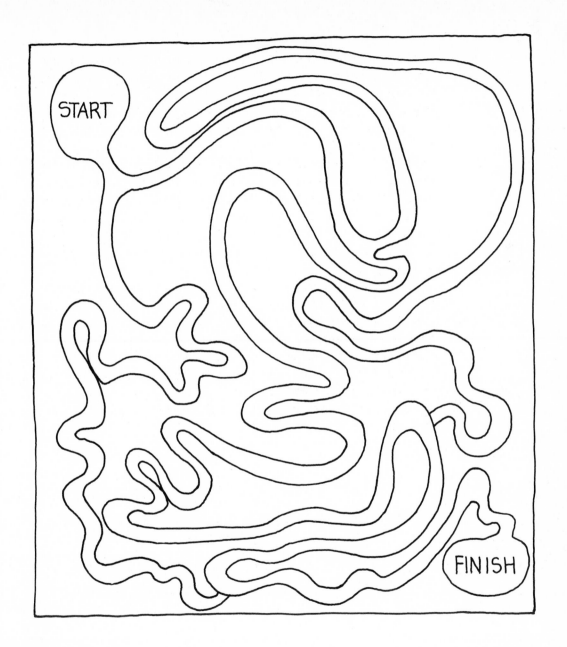

START

FINISH

JIGSAW PUZZLES

MATERIALS

photographs from magazines
or other sources
scissors
glue
oak tag or poster board
pencil
envelope

Commercial jigsaws offer fine visual exercise for children. But there are advantages to making your own puzzles. Your own handmade puzzles are personal, unique, and therefore special. They are also cheap and easy to construct, which is a lucky thing. Sooner or later your child will lose a crucial puzzle piece. When you have made your own puzzle, this is no great tragedy. Just throw out the ruined puzzle and make a new one.

Consider the usefulness of puzzle-playing for a child like Gloria. Gloria had tremendous difficulties in visual perception. If 13 was written on a page, she saw 31. When asked to copy:

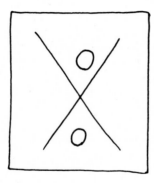   she produced:

Although she was in first grade and should have been able to write her name clearly, Gloria's signature looked something like this:

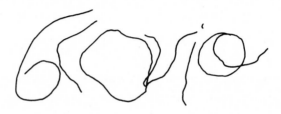

When a first-grader consistently reverses numbers, has trouble copying simple designs, and can't control her handwriting, it's a good guess that she's experiencing problems in visual perception. Gloria needed to anchor her visual world—she needed visual exercises.

Consequently, we spent our time together playing with puzzles. On jigsaw days I brought a selection of photographs into school. These were primarily magazine photos, but any other interesting pictures will do. Just make sure the pictures are at least 6" x 8". Gloria picked her favorite photograph and we glued it to a piece of oak tag. This has to be done carefully: the back of the photograph must be completely covered with a very thin layer of glue, then pressed onto oak tag. It's easier if the oak tag is somewhat larger than the photograph.

Once the glue is dry, the jigsawing begins. Turn the oak tag blank side up. Now draw the puzzle design on the blank surface. Initially I did the drawing for Gloria. Once she got the hang of how puzzle pieces link together, I let her draw. Here are two different puzzle drawings:

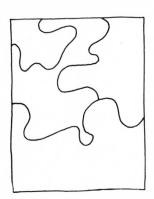 

As you can see, the puzzles don't need to have lots of pieces. When your child draws, make sure the design stays simple. Remember that anything drawn has to be cut with scissors—and then put back together again.

I did the cutting myself at first. When I was confident that Gloria could do a good job, I let her use the scissors, too. She tried her best to cut on the lines, but if she made a few errors, that was OK. I made sure that bits of the puzzles didn't get snipped away completely.

As soon as the puzzle was cut, Gloria was ready to try her hand at putting it back together. She shuffled and shifted the pieces around. She tried to see if

would fit with

She tested one shape against another. After some hard work, the puzzle was solved. She didn't think of puzzle-solving as a lesson in seeing, but it was.

Afterward, we broke the puzzle up and put it away in an envelope for another day. By the end of the school year, Gloria had made about fifteen different puzzles. I can't count the number of times those puzzles were put together and taken apart.

What effect did puzzle-playing (and a few other games) have on Gloria's problems with reading? Throughout first grade and most of second grade, Gloria couldn't read more than a handful of words. Then, suddenly, the perceptual training seemed to click. Gloria's visual world fell into place. She started to read fluently. Presto!—a year and a half later.

*B*LINDFOLD DRAWING gives your child a unique visual experience that comes from drawing in a decidedly strange manner. There are two rules. Rule one: the person who draws is blindfolded. Most children enjoy being blindfolded. If your child doesn't, he can just close his eyes. Rule two: the person who draws never lets his pencil leave the paper. If you're drawing a head and want to put in the eyes, nose, and mouth, you must draw them with a single line.

MATERIALS

cloth or scarf for blindfolding
paper
pencil

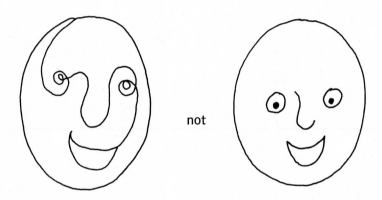

not

I'll never forget Toni's reaction when I explained BLINDFOLD DRAWING. "I can't draw with my eyes blindfolded!" she exclaimed. "I can't draw without lifting my pencil! That's crazy!"

"I know you can't draw good drawings with your eyes closed. But you can draw silly ones. I'll go first so you can see how silly my drawings come out." I asked what she'd like me to draw. She proposed a cat. I tied a scarf around my head, covering my eyes. I told her how I was trying to imagine a cat, to visualize the whole cat in my mind. Then I began to draw. Toni started to giggle. I knew my drawing must look pretty ridiculous. After I had finished, I took off the scarf. Then we both had to giggle.

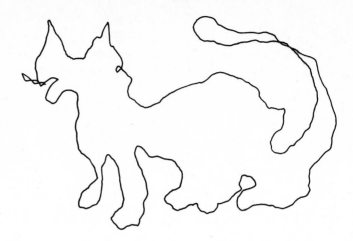

My drawing proved that beauty was not the point.

Now it was Toni's turn. After she positioned her pencil on the paper, I blindfolded her. In the beginning, Toni drew simple objects (eggs, bowls) and shapes (squares, triangles). Once she felt at ease, she drew more complicated pictures (animals, houses, automobiles). Whatever she drew, I told her first to create the drawing in her imagination. Once the drawing was in her mind, she could start moving her pencil.

BLINDFOLD DRAWING became one of Toni's favorite activities. I think she liked it so much because for every picture she squiggled out, I scrawled a clumsy drawing of my own. Children do love seeing grownups make a mess of things. For my part, I loved seeing Toni exercise her visual imagination. By mentally picturing images of eggs and cats, she was training her ability to recall visual images of all sorts. Words are visual images too, of course, and the ability to recall them is one of the main skills in reading.

*H*ow many baby strollers did

you see today? You probably have no idea. People don't walk around keeping track of the number of strollers they pass. If you and your child took a FIND IT walk, however, and baby strollers were the object of your FIND IT attention, you would indeed count strollers. You and your child would walk along the street scanning and scouting, on the lookout for baby strollers. This intense observation accounts for FIND IT's value as a visual game.

Just about anything can serve as an object for your search, from people in blue sweaters to dogs on leashes. Of course, what you look for depends on where you look. In the city it makes sense to look for people carrying briefcases or grocery bags; during a walk in the country, look for yellow wildflowers or birds in flight.

Both you and your child can actively look for the FIND IT object. Sometimes you may have to bite your tongue to make sure your child sees the wildflowers for himself.

FIND IT

There's an old game for car trips that is basically a variation of FIND IT. In this game, automobile passengers try to find every letter of the alphabet. The game begins when someone in the car spots a sign or license plate with the letter A. Then the search is on for B, next C, and so forth until you come to Z (Z is awfully hard to find). This is a cooperative alphabet game, but it can also become a contest. In that case, each player hunts for his own alphabet. When a contestant spies a letter he needs, he announces, "A on the yellow billboard!" No one else can use that yellow-billboard A. Whoever reaches Z first, wins. If the trip ends before anyone gets to Z, then the person closest to the end of the alphabet wins.

Your car-ride search needn't be limited to alphabet letters. Set up mini-contests: in the next five miles, who can find the most out-of-state license plates? the most cars with more than four people inside? Fords? sports cars? (Zip—there goes Porsche number 3!)

These kinds of games may not seem impressive, but they help children see more accurately. For some children, that's crucial; for all children, it's helpful. And at the same time, these games are very entertaining.

PICTURE MEMORY

*T*his game lets you use family photos in a new way. Pick a snapshot and show it to your child. Let him study it for a minute or two. Then take it away and ask questions. What color pants did Daddy have on? How many swimmers were in the pool? What kind of shoes was Tim wearing? Are there two, three, or four trees in the picture? After a few questions show your child the picture again and discuss his answers. Then let him choose a picture for you to study. You'll be the one who has to squirm and answer difficult questions.

Family photos aren't the only pictures you can use. Magazine photographs work just as well. Ask your child to identify the color of the sweater in the men's wear ad. What the girl is holding in the cornflakes ad? How many birds are flying over the ocean in the travel ad? You might try this game on a bus, street, subway, or anywhere else you see picture ads.

You can also use book illustrations. Take a break when you're reading aloud. Let your child study one of the illustrations. Then ask a question or two. How many rabbits are pulling Pooh out of the rabbit hole? What color are the bows on Cinderella's gown? How many cookies are in Hansel's hands?

Just make sure these questions are a game, not an exam. Nothing could be worse than to make your child live in an atmosphere of permanent quiz. It's up to you to create a mood that's intellectually stimulating, not daunting; fun, not nerve-racking. Easy does it.

MATERIALS

photographs and/or book illustrations

HOW DO I LOOK?

Can you reproduce something that you see? If you can, you're visualizing accurately. Try this with your child. Strike a pose, the more theatrical the better. Then ask your child to copy you. He should try to stand, sit, or lie exactly like you. If your arm is bent, if your leg is twisted, if you are frowning, if your tongue is sticking out, his should be, too. Start with simple poses. Later on, get more complicated. Demand more. If your head is tilted at 50°, his should be 50°, not 45°. Naturally your child will want to be the leader, too. He'll want to strike poses for you to copy. And, naturally, you must do as you're told.

After copy-catting each other for a while, try this variation of HOW DO I LOOK? Strike a new pose. Let your child observe you. Then tell him to close his eyes. While his eyes are closed, make a change. You can relax an arm, move a leg, or unbutton your sweater. Once you make a move, sit very still and tell your child to open his eyes. His job is to discover how you changed. After he guesses, tell him if he's right or wrong.

Make some changes that are easy to see: put your hand behind your back, uncross your legs, change expressions from smile to frown. Then try changes that are hard to see: move your hand from your lap to your side, untie your shoes, turn your head. And try out a few itsy-bitsy changes: remove an earring, tousle your hair, shift your foot a few inches to the right. Needless to say, your child will want to take turns being the leader in this version, too.

One of the nice things about HOW DO I LOOK? games is that you can play them anywhere. You may look strange posing on a bus or in a doctor's office, but so what? If someone stares, suggest that he buy a copy of this book. Then he can play reading games with his own child.

SET THE TABLE is similar to HOW DO I LOOK? To play SET THE TABLE you must get two paper bags and fill them identically with ten or fifteen small objects. The bags might each include a spool of thread, an eraser, a checker, a fork, a pencil, a safety pin, a sock, a nail, an envelope, a paper clip, and a baseball card. Just be sure that both bags have the same collection of items.

Once the bags are full, give one to your child and sit side by side with him at the table. Take three or four objects out of your bag and arrange them in a design on the table. Your child looks at this table arrangement, takes the identical objects from his own paper bag, and duplicates the design.

MATERIALS

two paper bags
a variety of small objects
(you'll want two of each
object—two pencil sharpeners,
two bobby pins,
two model cars, and so on)

my arrangement

a good enough copy

This is trickier than it seems. Your child will be seeing the design at a different angle from yours—he's not sitting in front of it. He has to visualize the arrangement as if it were directly in front of him, and then re-create this design. If he has trouble doing this, get up from your seat and let him sit there. He can study your design from the appropriate angle and then return to his own seat and copy what he saw. That's the game.

Switch roles. Let your child set the table; you copy his design. Eventually, you can make the game harder by adding more pieces to the design. Instead of four pieces, set the table with five, six, seven, or eight. It takes a lot of visual skill to reproduce a crowded design.

An alternate version of SET THE TABLE begins the same way but ends differently. Take three or four objects from your bag and arrange them on the table.

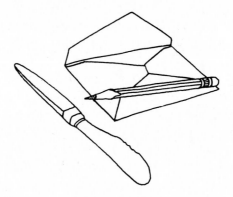

Give your child a chance to study the table. Then tell him to close his eyes. Make a change, or perhaps two changes, in the original arrangement. For instance, take the pencil away and move the knife to the other side of the envelope.

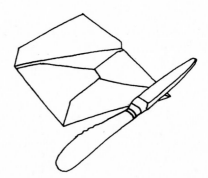

When your child opens his eyes, tell him how many changes you've made. If he sees the changes right away, congratulate him. If he doesn't, be reassuring—and make the next changes more obvious. When your child understands the game, switch roles. The child makes the arrangement, changes it, and you must identify what the changes were.

If your child shows great skill playing this game, increase the number of starting objects. But don't go overboard, making the game so hard it's no longer fun. Having a good time with this game is more important than cluttering a table top with envelopes and safety pins.

You might try playing SET THE TABLE at mealtimes. Sit down to lunch and arrange your sandwich, juice, apple, and napkin on the table. Tell your child to study your lunch, then close his eyes. Before asking him to look again, take a bite of your sandwich, hide the apple in your lap, or crumple the napkin. When his eyes are open, he must say what happened to your lunch. Call this food for thought.

TWO DRAWING GAMES

MATERIALS

paper
pencils
crayons

Here are two drawing games on the pattern of HOW DO I LOOK? and SET THE TABLE. The first game is a copying game. Start by drawing a simple design with geometric patterns and shapes.

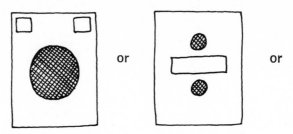 or

Show your child the drawing and let him try his best to copy it. In copying, he'll be making all sorts of visual judgments. "Is this the right shape? Is this the right size? Did I put everything in the right position? Let me check Daddy's drawing and see."

Don't expect, and tell your child not to expect, perfect copies. If a child can manage a reasonable approximation of a drawing, he's doing a terrific job. As he gets better at copying, you can make the original design a bit harder to duplicate. Do this by adding more shapes and placing them randomly on the page.

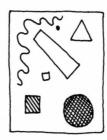

This, for example, is a very hard drawing to copy. A child's eye must be very well developed to copy such a drawing with any accuracy.

When your child is used to copying drawings, try a second drawing game. Draw a picture. Let your child study the drawing.

Then tell him to close his eyes. While his eyes are closed, make a change in your drawing. Your child opens his eyes, studies the drawing, and tries to locate the change.

Your drawings can be realistic or abstract. Whichever you choose, start with simple designs and make the changes fairly obvious.

can become

After a while, changes can be more subtle.

becomes

Or you can ask your child to find more than one change.

I made three changes in this drawing. Can you find them all?

When your child gets expert, try starting with a complicated drawing. Then any change you make is automatically more diffi-cult to detect.

 becomes

A child's visual memory must be remarkably sharp to pick up the differences between these two drawings. When a child achieves such eagle-eye vision, it's something to celebrate.

*H*ere's another drawing game, which is much harder than the others I've described. This game exercises the ability to memorize, as well as the ability to copy.

Start by drawing a picture composed of geometric shapes and simple designs. Your child watches as you draw. When you are finished, cover your drawing, give your child a piece of paper, and let him try to re-create the drawing.

Stick with simple drawings until your child is perfectly comfortable with the game. Here are some examples.

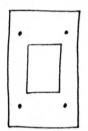 or 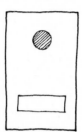 or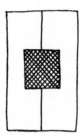

In time, you can add more difficult drawings:

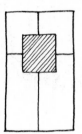 or  or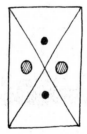

And more difficult still:

 or  or

You should keep to symmetrical, repetitive patterns with just a few colors. Eventually your child will be able to reproduce complicated designs of this sort. You can help a child remember the design if you talk while you draw.

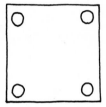

"First I'm drawing four blue circles."

"I'm filling in the top circles with blue."

"Now I'll add a red square."

"I'll color the square green."

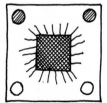

"I think I'll draw green lines coming out all over the square."

There is something you can do to make this hard game even harder. Have your child close his eyes while you draw the original. When he opens his eyes, he is confronted with the completed drawing. This makes copying much more difficult.

From time to time, playing this drawing game and the others I've described, I've switched roles with children: I've let them do the original drawing and I've copied from memory. Unfortunately, whenever I've made this switch, it's been a disaster. The children make crazy, impossible drawings. Sometimes this is funny; usually, it's annoying. That's why I don't switch drawing any more. Still, you might have better luck. Your child may be more reasonable than most. If you want to try it, go right ahead.

LETTER CONTEST

MATERIALS

books
optional:
a paper bag
pen
scissors
paper

Gregory loved contests. So when I realized that he needed vision exercise, I invented LETTER CONTEST. I worried at first that the game was too simple to capture Gregory's imagination. Fortunately, there was no such problem. He was fascinated.

The game consists of hunting for an individual letter inside a given paragraph. I asked Gregory to pick a favorite letter. He said "G". He wanted to know why I was asking, but I didn't tell him yet. Instead I opened a book of fairy tales at random. I told Gregory that a paragraph is a block of print that goes from one indentation to the next, and I showed him a couple of examples. Then he picked a paragraph. The paragraph contained lots of difficult words, and he was worried that I would make him read. But LETTER CONTEST isn't about reading. The idea is to count all the G's (or whatever other letter you've chosen) that appear in a single paragraph. I told Gregory to go through the paragraph word by word, letter by letter, looking for G, both capital and lower case.

Gregory placed his finger under the first word. His face scrunched up in concentration. All of his ability to focus on visual images was being called upon. He'd have to identify each letter to locate the G's. Slowly his finger moved along the page.

In olden times there was a King, who had behind his palace a beautiful garden in which there was a tree that bore golden apples. When the apples were getting ripe they were counted, but on the very next morning one was missing. This was told to the King, and he ordered that a watch should be kept every night beneath the tree.

Gregory counted nine G's. Now it was my turn. I picked P and scrutinized the same paragraph. I found seven P's (carefully showing them to Gregory as I counted). Nine G's to seven P's—Gregory won the contest.

We decided to take a second look at the same paragraph, only this time we'd hunt for new letters. Gregory picked A. I picked O.

Gregory slaughtered me. He found nineteen A's. I found twelve O's. Gregory thumbed through the book, looking for a new paragraph. When he saw one he liked, we started again. Gregory decided to look for F's. I picked D's. This time I won the contest.

Actually, I had a lot of control in this game. I knew something Gregory didn't. In a contest between D and F, I knew that D will usually win. If I had wanted to be sure to lose the game, I would have picked Q or X. This ruined the competitive aspect of LETTER CONTEST for me, since I could decide beforehand if I wanted to win or lose. To keep the game suspenseful, I changed the way we selected contest letters. I took twenty-one small strips of paper and wrote out all the letters of the alphabet except J, Q, V, X, and Z (which occur too seldom to be much fun in this game). I mixed up the strips and put them in a paper bag. Gregory shook the bag, stuck in his hand, and pulled out an M. I came up with a B. These were our contest letters.

You can use any kind of printed material for this game, including children's books, magazines, and newspapers. Sometimes Gregory and I hunted for letters in one of the books from my own shelf. The print in my books was small, but Gregory could handle it, at least for a paragraph or two. The extra effort was worth it to him. He felt very proud using a thick, grown-up book for his work. Someday he'll read Tolstoy for himself. But now, with a gigantic volume of *War and Peace* on his lap, he was happy searching for B's, F's, and T's.

SAME AND DIFFERENT

MATERIALS

strips of paper
pen or pencil

José was a fairly good reader who nevertheless stumbled over look-alike words. English is filled with look-alike words—*where* and *there*, *went* and *want*, *left* and *felt*, *saw* and *was*, *what* and *want*. José confused them all. Because he was confused, he got frustrated; when he was frustrated, he got angry. But confusion, frustration, and anger are not conducive to good reading. José needed help: above all, practice in looking at similar-looking groups of letters and in quickly identifying the difference between them. For José, SAME AND DIFFERENT was just what the reading teacher ordered.

To play SAME AND DIFFERENT, I needed a pile of paper strips. I cut these from sheets of blank paper and drew a line down the middle of each strip. Then I held the strip so that José couldn't see it. I wrote two sets of letters, one set on each side of the line. Sometimes these were identical sets, sometimes they were different:

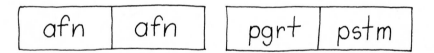

Now the strip was ready to show to José. First I held it writing-side down, so that José couldn't see the letters. Then I flipped it over for one or two seconds.

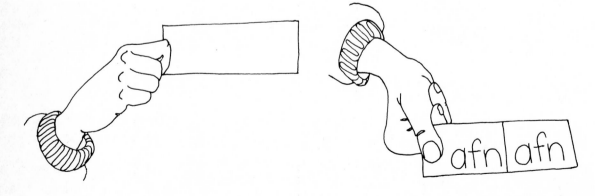

After this quick movement, I turned the strip writing-side down again and asked José, "Were the two sets of letters the same or different?" He gave his answer, and I flipped over the strip. That way he could check his own answers. José looked at strip after strip. Sometimes I wrote three, or four, or even five letters on each side of the line. Sometimes I wrote sets of numbers instead of letters. Sometimes I wrote words. José didn't have to read these words. He only needed to tell me if the two sides of the strip were the same or different. Of course, if he started to read the words, I didn't stop him.

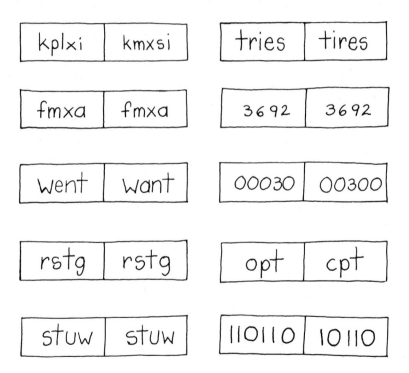

kplxi	kmxsi
fmxa	fmxa
went	want
rstg	rstg
stuw	stuw

tries	tires
3692	3692
00030	00300
opt	cpt
110110	10110

Strip by strip, José's confusion over *where*s and *there*s, *who*s and *how*s, *stop*s and *spot*s faded into the past, along with his anger and frustration.

chapter 3.

Word Games

In the end, we learn to read by memorizing thousands of words. Children accomplish a large part of this memorization in the first six grades. By third grade, children have already been introduced to over three thousand words, of which they are expected to memorize a fair number.

Memorization takes practice, and the single best kind of practice is reading itself. The second best is playing lots of word games. The games in this chapter will get your child to play board games with words and to enjoy vocabulary flash cards. By and large, the games drill children on basic vocabulary. Drill is boring; but when drill comes in the form of a game like bingo, it's really not so bad. Your child may not like every game in this chapter, but one or another should meet with a good reception.

*T*his is a terrific board game for teaching color words. The board, drawn on a large piece of paper, oak tag, or poster board looks like this:

MATERIALS

large piece of paper, oak tag, or poster board (at least 11" x 14")

index cards

box of crayons

pen

two little toys or objects for game tokens (for example, a quarter, a paper clip, a checker)

or even like this:

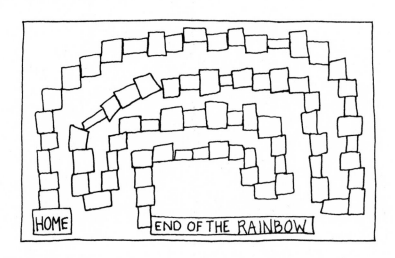

The first square is "home." The last square is the "end of the rainbow." The in-between squares are colored at random white, black, red, blue, yellow, green, purple, orange, brown, gray, and pink. Your child might enjoy helping you make this board.

You also need a pile of fifteen or twenty index cards, labeled in black and white with the names of all the colors on the board: *white*, *black*, *red*, *blue*, *yellow*, *green*, *purple*, *orange*, *brown*, *gray*, and *pink*. There should be three other cards, which say: "miss a turn"; "go back to orange"; "go back to blue." These are "terrible trouble" cards.

This is a race game: both players start with a token at "home" and draw cards in order to race around the board. You each draw a card in turn and move your token to the next corresponding space on the board. When you draw a "terrible trouble" card, you have to do what it says. Eventually you'll get to the bottom of the pile of cards, and then you must reshuffle the stack and start over. You and your child keep reading colors until somebody gets to the "end of the rainbow." End of the rainbow—end of the game. Meanwhile your child has had a lot of practice reading the names of colors.

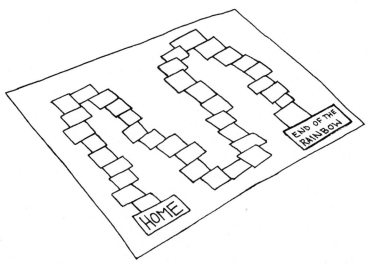

*H*ere's a word game I played with a boy named Steve. In order to play, I had to make a deck of fifteen vocabulary flash cards. I wrote the flash card words on index cards. Then I needed a WORD LADDER playing board. The board was a "ladder" with twelve steps, drawn on oak tag or paper.

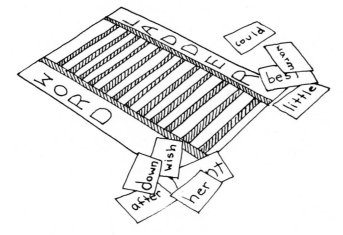

To play the game, Steve turned over one flash card at a time and read the words aloud. Every time he read a word correctly, he moved his token up a step on the ladder. To get to the top he needed to read twelve out of fifteen words correctly. That was victory.

Picking the words is your main task in preparing WORD LADDER. Use the "List of Important Words" in the appendices. These words make up a basic reading vocabulary for young readers. With a very beginning reader, you will want to choose exclusively from the beginning list. As your child gains skill, you can increase the difficulty of the game a little by throwing in a few words from the intermediate list. Later you might spice things up with words from the toughie list. You can judge how hard to make the words by how well the child does in this game: he should be able to win, but not too easily.

Write each word on an individual card. You can make several packs of fifteen cards and alternate them when you play.

Before starting the game, read the words with your child to accustom him to them. Next time you use the same pack of cards, this won't be necessary.

Playing with Steve one day, I selected the following combination of words. Three words came from the beginning list: *her, down, play.* I took seven words from the intermediate list: *little, could, something, after, white, went, want.* From the toughie list I selected: *wish, drink, best, warm, thought.*

Since these were new words, we went through the pile together. This gave Steve a sort of dry run. Now we were ready to start the game. Steve picked a game token. He happened to love model cars, so I kept one around to be used as a token in our board games. Here is the play-by-play account of Steve's drive up the word ladder.

He took the top card, which was *after.* This was not one of the simplest words in the pack. Even so, he read it without difficulty. Steve took his first step up the ladder. Next he picked *her,* an easy word. He took a second step up the ladder. He wasn't able to read *could* and *warm.* Then he drew *play* and *something.* They were a breeze. He struggled sounding out *drink* and *white,* but got them right. Now he was six steps up the ladder. He turned over the next card. It was *thought,* a difficult word that couldn't be sounded out. Steve tried to remember, but was stuck. At this point he had missed three words. Steve knew he couldn't make any more errors if he was going to win the game. He turned over *down* and *little.* He was able to read both. Now he was eight steps up the ladder. Could he climb four more steps without making mistakes? He turned over *want* and misread it as *went.* This was a tricky error, but an error nonetheless. He had lost the game. We went through the rest of the cards anyway to see how high he could go. He missed one more word and got up ten of the twelve steps.

Now that he had more practice with the words, Steve was eager to try again. This time he not only remembered *went* and *thought*, but got to the top of the ladder with only two errors. I challenged him, "I bet you can't do that again. I bet the words will trick you this time." Steve took up the challenge. For a third time he started up the ladder and made it to the top again. More importantly, he was no longer sounding out words like *drink* and *white*; he could read them at sight. Also, he was starting to memorize words that can't be sounded out, such as *thought* and *could.* The game was working. Steve was learning flash-card words and enjoying it.

If you and your child like this game, why not keep a cigar box or shoe box filled with bundles of words on your game shelf? Suggest to your child that if he studies the words in his spare time, he'll do better at the game. And maybe he will study— anything's possible.

When a bundle becomes too easy, take time to gloat together over the number of words your child has learned. Let him have the pleasure of throwing those cinchy words away. Then replace the bundle with a new one.

WORD CONCEN-TRATION

MATERIALS

index cards

pen

Concentration is a popular card game with children and can be put to use in stretching your child's reading vocabulary. You need a deck of thirty word cards: fifteen words written on two cards each. These thirty cards are laid out, face down, on a table or floor. The goal of the game is to find as many word pairs as possible. Players flip over two cards in each turn. If a player turns over a matching pair of words, he gets to keep both cards. If the two cards don't match, they are both returned to face-down position. The players must try very hard to remember exactly where every word is located. The more a player remembers, the more word pairs he'll be able to find. With some children, you must encourage them to apply reason to the game and not trust solely to chance.

Here is part of a game Hilary and I played. We sat side by side at the table and I arranged the thirty cards in rows and columns in front of us. It's helpful to keep a neat arrangement of cards.

Hilary made the first move. She turned over a single card, picked at random. It said *house*, and she read this aloud. (I helped her read any word she didn't know.) Now she had to turn over a second card, any card. With luck, the second card would say *house*. If it did, she'd have a match. She turned over the second card, which said *picture*. No match. She kept the two cards face up for about fifteen seconds so we could concentrate and remember where they were located.

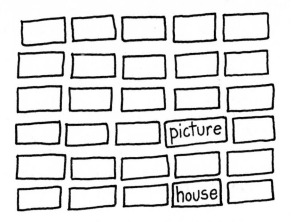

Then she turned the two cards face down, the way they were originally. It was my chance to turn over cards. First I turned over *city*. I read the card out loud. Then I turned over *house*. This wasn't the same *house* Hilary had found. It was the match she had hoped for.

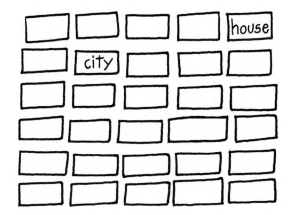

I left the two cards face up so we could study their position. Then I turned them face down. Now it was Hilary's turn to concentrate. Lucky Hilary: if she concentrated very hard, she'd remember the location of both *houses* and get a match. If she didn't, I'd have a chance to make the match myself. Hilary turned over her first card. It said *house*. All she had to do was remember where the other *house* was hiding. Could she do it? She turned over another card. *House* again! A brilliant move! Hilary's concentration had paid off. She picked up the two cards and kept them next to her. Because she'd found a match, she got to pick again. She turned over two more cards. They didn't match. Now it was my turn once more.

When the game ended, Hilary had nine word pairs and I had six. Hilary had very good concentration. Not everyone has such a superb memory, so be patient. The more you play, the better you'll get. Your child will get better too, which is more to the point. Another thing about WORD CONCENTRATION is that, although it moves slowly in the beginning, excitement grows as the game goes on.

WORD CONCENTRATION is a simple game to make. All you need is the deck of word cards. I suggest index cards cut in half. Then pick out fifteen words for your pairs. Use the appendix of "Important Words." Start with easy words. It's no trouble to increase the difficulty of the game; just replace words your child has learned with new ones. Once a child learns the words in the easy list, mix in a few intermediate and later a few toughie words. The deck can also grow gradually from thirty to forty cards. I think forty cards (twenty pairs) is as large a deck as you'll want to use—forty cards takes a powerful lot of concentration.

J ulio came to New York from Latin America in the summer between first and second grade. When he started classes, he was in a new school, without friends, and knew no English. Three months later he spoke English (and refused to speak anything else), had many friends, and was an old hand around school. Here was one very smart little boy. Naturally, during these first few months we put no pressure on him to read. We recognized that when he was ready he would learn to read with the same intensity with which he had learned to speak English. Sure enough, that's how it was. Julio started insisting, demanding to read. Not only that, he wanted to read as proficiently as his friends—right now!

I started working with Julio individually. I'm not sure I taught him. It was more that I poured out information and he drank it up. One of my primary goals with Julio was to help him memorize lots of reading words. To do this, I used games. In our months of work together, his favorite game was WORD BINGO. We must have played at least once a week for six or seven months.

WORD BINGO is a cousin of regular bingo. Each player has a bingo board made out of paper or oak tag and divided into twenty-five squares. The center square is "free." The other twenty-four squares have vocabulary words written in them. Each playing board has the same twenty-four words, but the words are located in different squares.

MATERIALS

paper,
oak tag, or poster board
pen
colored construction paper
index cards
optional: storage box

no	good	to	may	play
did	who	some	yes	red
and	ran	FREE	little	cow
like	ride	have	work	down
time	one	her	big	me

did	her	who	work	time
have	like	big	red	ran
one	play	FREE	yes	may
to	down	cow	me	ride
and	little	good	some	no

The twenty-four words are also written on individual index cards. You need, in addition, a pile of small squares of colored construction paper to use as bingo markers.

To begin playing, Julio and I each chose a board. We immediately covered our respective free spaces (the square in the middle) with bingo markers. Then I shuffled the deck of twenty-four index cards. Julio picked the top card and read the word aloud—with help from me if he needed it. We scanned our bingo boards until we found this word, and then both covered that square with a marker. Julio picked a second card, and we proceeded as before. The first player to cover five squares in a row—either vertically, horizontally, or diagonally—calls out "BINGO!" and wins the game.

no	▨	▨	may	play
did	who	some	▨	red
and	ran	▨	little	▨
like	▨	have	work	▨
time	▨	▨	▨	▨

did	▨	who	work	time
have	like	▨	red	ran
▨	play	▨	▨	may
▨	▨	▨	▨	▨
and	little	▨	some	no

B I N G O

62

Bingo words can be selected from the appendix of "Important Words." I started Julio with easy words. Once he was secure with words from one game, I made a new bingo set with new words. I never threw out boards or index cards, but kept them in a box labeled WORD BINGO. That way I had a variety of bingo games for Julio to use, some with new words, some with old. Using these different bingo sets, Julio learned dozens and dozens of easy, intermediate, and toughie words. In due time Julio's demands were met. He was reading just as well as his friends. WORD BINGO wasn't solely responsible for Julio's success, but it did play a part.

Although bingo is fine to play with two people, the game is even more suspenseful when there are more players. WORD BINGO is therefore terrific for the whole family. Just make enough boards for everybody. Maybe you can recruit someone to help you do this, an older child perhaps, who will benefit from helping you write the words. The words you pick should be appropriate for the least experienced reader in the household. Then let every child (adults, too, for that matter) take turns reading the bingo cards. One more point—this game goes very well with popcorn.

GOOFY SENTENCES

What would your child think if you asked him to read this sentence?

An orange barked to get strong.

He'd probably think it was pretty funny. What would he think of an activity that consisted of constructing and reading dozens of such crazy sentences? If you guess he'd think it a great idea, then keep reading.

On page 66 there are twenty sentence beginnings, twenty sentence middles, and twenty sentence endings. Start by copying the sentence beginnings on index cards (you can use half or quarter cards for this purpose). Mix up the cards. Then keep them together with a rubber band. Copy the sentence middles, mix them up, and bind them, too. Do the same thing with the sentence endings. Now you have three piles of cards.

When you're ready to play, place the cards—beginnings, middles, and endings—in front of the child. Explain that in this game he'll get to create and read goofy sentences. All he has to do is pick three cards—one from each pile—put them together, and read the results. Sometimes these parts fit together sensibly:

| Mom | was in a hurry | to go to work. |

More often they don't:

| Mom | lives in a cave | with milk. |

or

| Mom | flies quickly | with milk. |

64

Sometimes the fit is not at all fitting:

or

These nonsentences don't ruin the game. Just shrug them off. "Boy, that doesn't make sense at all. It's not even a sentence."

When you and your child have finished goofing off for the day, wrap up the sentence parts in their rubber bands and store them for another time. These twenty beginnings, twenty middles, and twenty endings allow a child to create 8,000 different sentence combinations. That should keep him giggling for a while. While he giggles he'll get lots of practice reading words and phrases. Feel free to add your own sentence parts. Your child might have some good ideas, too. Just combine new cards with the originals and see what goofy sentences pop up.

By the way, this game also gives a child an early taste for sentence structure and grammar. Later in his school work he'll learn about sentences in a more exacting way, but this is a nice beginning.

BEGINNINGS	MIDDLES	ENDINGS
The little boy	rode a bicycle	to the store.
Dad	ran from the house	to catch a bus.
Mom	was in a hurry	to go to work.
My teacher	waited	to get my work.
The horse	ran through the woods	to get to the ranch.
My cat	wanted	to catch a mouse.
The dog	barked	to scare a stranger.
The brown chair	was there	so I could sit down.
The big lion	slept in the woods	while I ran away.
A baby elephant	looked for his mom	in the jungle.
My friend	ate apples	to get strong.
An orange	grows	in the sun.
The cat	cleans himself	by licking.
The bear	lives in a cave	to keep warm.
The boat	sails down the river	without stopping.
The woman	opens the door	to the house.
The man	catches fish	in the river.
The sofa	is on the floor	by the window.
My cup	is filled	with milk.
The bird	flies quickly	to his nest.

*L*inda needed to look at new vocabulary words over and over before they sank in. I used to write out one sentence after another containing the new words and have her read them as a method of repetition. But these sentences got very boring.

"I'm tired of sentences," she complained. "They're too easy. I could read them upside down." This gave me an idea. "OK," I answered, "let's see if you can read this one all mixed up." I wrote a new sentence: *He likes driving in the country.* Then, with scissors, I cut the sentence into individual words:

I took the individual words and mixed them up. Put back on the table, they read:

"Here's a mix-up," I said. "Can you make a sentence out of it?" Her eyes lit up. Boredom was gone.

First she read all the words. I helped her with hard ones. Linda needed, and got, help with words throughout the game. I also gave her a clue: sentences begin with capital letters and end with periods, exclamation points, or question marks. I showed Linda these features. Some sentences have more than one capital letter (*Did Mary take a coat?*). In these cases, she'd have to choose the right beginning words. The present example contained only one capital letter. She set up the first and last words.

Now she had to make a sentence. She moved the words. First she tried:

| He | driving | in | the | likes | country. |

No good. She tried:

| He | likes | the | driving | in | country. |

She read it—almost, but not quite. She waited a moment. Smiling, she turned to the cards and rearranged them:

| He | likes | driving | in | the | country. |

SUCCESS!

At this point, Linda had read the words no less than five times. The two words I was trying to teach her, *driving* and *country*, were now familiar. She'd had a great time. And incidentally, she had learned something about the structure of sentences.

You can make sentences as easy as *I like cats.* You can make them as difficult as *The Princess climbed to the top of the world's highest mountain.* When the sentences are long, group the words together:

| The princess | climbed | to the | top |
| of the | world's | highest mountain. |

Feel free to make up any sentence that strikes your fancy. Be
serious:

The | boy | cried and | cried because |

he cut | his | knee.

Be silly:

The boy | cut his | knee | chasing | a big |

kangaroo | up a | tree.

Be sillier:

The kangaroo | ate | five | jars of |

pickles | for lunch.

Be silliest:

Peter | picked eight | pickles | for the |

kangaroo's | green pickle | birthday |

pie   surprise.

Here are twenty sentences you can use, arranged more or less in order of difficulty:

Here | I | am.

The boy | can ride | a bike.

I | must | eat a | hot dog.

The | girl | has a | green | frog.

I am | king | of the | world.

She | works | in the | city.

The lion | went | shopping | for hats.

This | elephant | just stepped | on my | toe.

The | baby | ate all | the | birthday cake.

The | frog | just | turned | into a | queen.

My | brown | horse | sings | cowboy | songs.

Follow that masked man to Kalamazoo.

Would you write me a letter?

The octopus and the whale played baseball.

The bear wanted to fly like a bird.

Grandmother rode a pretty camel to the party.

The giant cried when he was stung by the bee.

My teacher thought she saw a goat in school.

The monkey rode on a train to see his sister drink a milkshake.

The squirrel went to the beach with a beautiful rhinoceros.

MATERIALS

index cards
pen
blank paper

Flash cards help children read new words. Children look at the words over and over, either in games or drill, until they remember them. That's fine. ZIP CARDS is a more advanced game. It encourages a child to see words and phrases and recognize them in the blink of an eye—zippily.

I've found that, in the supersonic age, ZIP CARDS delights children. They love the idea of becoming speed readers. That's the way it was with Cathy. Cathy was already doing well in reading and was thrilled to take on a new challenge. Therefore I produced my handy box of ZIP CARDS. Initially I turned over the cards slowly, one at a time, and let Cathy read them at a reasonable pace. If there were words or phrases she couldn't fathom, I threw them out and chose new ones that gave her no trouble.

Then it was time to zip. I held up the first card and put it down in a single motion. Cathy could see the word for about one second. She had to say the word aloud. Did she say it correctly? The card went in the zip pile. Did she say it incorrectly, or was she unable even to guess what word it was? That card went in the unzip pile.

After she tried reading all the cards, we counted how many she zipped and how many she didn't. This was her score. We wrote the score on a paper scoreboard. Each time we went through the deck, we marked her score on the board. Cathy loved seeing how she got better and better at speed reading.

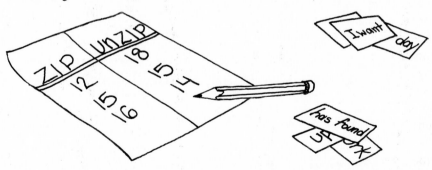

In general, I didn't go through the deck more than three or four times in a single sitting. Instead I'd wait for another day and play again, either with the same deck or with a new selection of cards.

Don't feel your child has to read each card every time. ZIP CARDS is helpful even if the child makes lots of mistakes. It gets him into the habit of reading words and phrases in one gulp.

How to make a deck for ZIP CARDS? You'll need thirty index cards. On each card, write an Important Word from the appendix at the back—starting with simple words, of course, and using more difficult ones as your child gets more skillful. On some of the cards, write whole phrases. You can make the phrases up, or use the list that follows:

PHRASES FOR ZIP CARDS

do not	play ball	sister wins
I am	with father	all day
they are	will think	all night
big kiss	has made	one hug
at school	magic wish	mother cat
so long	will look	would go
went away	go away	so much
small car	at once	if I cry
little boy	I love	what to do
home run	did not go	has found
dogs bark	with me	they laugh
we are mad	will play	tree house
girl giant	when I read	I want
in the water	what I want	baby mouse
come home	good work	on the floor
toy store	can live	will the ghost
fly up here	has come back	want to go
on the chair	chocolate milk	street light
funny face	he said	bike ride
crazy about	you will like	you will do
stop fires	I am going	her brother
at home	huge elephants	too far
the yellow hat	jump up	birthday surprise

PART TWO

Games for
Learning Sounds

chapter 4.

Games for the Ear

Imagine that your child continually asked you to speak louder. What if he couldn't hear what other people could hear perfectly well? You'd be concerned; you'd arrange for a hearing test. Now suppose that your child hears what you say, but forgets what he is told, mixes up information, or must be given instructions over and over again before he understands. Should you be concerned about his hearing? Perhaps you should. People experience two kinds of hearing problems. The first kind, the one we all know about, exists when a person has trouble hearing sounds. The second kind occurs when someone has trouble ordering, remembering, or understanding the sounds he hears. These are problems in *perceptual* hearing. Problems in perceptual hearing are just as real as, though less disabling than, any other hearing difficulty.

In order for a child to sound out words, he or she must have good perceptual hearing. If a child can't perceive subtle differences between sounds, he won't be able to differentiate the *d*-sound from the *t*-sound. If a child has a poor memory for sounds, he'll have a hard time remembering which sounds go with what letters. If he can't blend separate sounds into words or confuses the order of sounds, when he tries to sound out *slide* he may come up with *side, site, slid,* or even *lice.* A child who experiences any of these problems is going to have trouble learning to read.

The games in this chapter help increase children's perceptual abilities. When children find it hard to remember letter sounds, their memories can be stretched if they learn riddles. When children can't differentiate letter sounds, mastering tongue twisters and jump-rope chants helps increase their sensitivity to sounds. When children have trouble hearing individual letter sounds and blending sounds into words, it's helpful to have them talk in "strange," artificial ways. "Strange talk" forces them to listen more carefully and develops their ability to manipulate sounds.

All children can benefit from these games, by the way, not just children with problems in hearing. Everyone can use a little sharpening of perceptual skills.

DO THIS, DO THAT

Gail couldn't follow directions. Even a simple request like "Get your workbook and a pencil" left her confused.

"What do you want me to get? . . . My pencil and what else? . . . I have my reading book; should I get my workbook, too? . . ."

Gail wasn't trying to avoid work. She wasn't even trying to annoy me. She had a problem in listening—a problem that affected her ability to read along with her ability to follow directions.

One game that helped her was DO THIS, DO THAT. This is a very bossy game, a little more complicated than Simon Says. I ordered Gail around. She had to follow my orders to a T. If this doesn't sound fun, it's only because you haven't heard the commands Gail had to obey. For instance:

"Stick out your tongue, wiggle your fingers."

"Shake my hand, jump in the air."

"Jump in a circle, yell as loud as you can."

"Skip to the window, climb on the chair, clap your hands."

"Take off your shoe, hop to the door, shake your head."

I gave Gail three chances to follow these instructions correctly. If after a third try she still confused them, we went on to a new set of orders.

Once Gail could reliably follow instructions that included three consecutive things to do, I made the game a little tougher: I added a "forgetting time." Forgetting time was a silent moment after I gave instructions. It lasted anywhere from five seconds to half a minute. Obviously, the longer the forgetting time, the harder it was for Gail to follow the instructions. Gail knew our forgetting time was over when I let loose with a loud "GO!"

Another way to make the game harder is to add more instructions. One glorious day Gail successfully followed four separate instructions:

"Turn in a circle, wiggle your whole body, jump to the bookshelf, meow like a cat."

On another day she actually reached five. Some children can do six, and those with extraordinary memories can occasionally re-member seven instructions.

"Shake all over, take giant steps to the window, take baby steps to the door, shake one leg, jump up and down."

"Tap your feet, make a loud noise, say hello, pretend you're a monkey, touch your nose, wiggle your fingers."

Orders can also get very specific. For instance, instead of tell-ing Gail to touch her ear, I told her to touch her right ear with her left hand. Such exacting instructions kept Gail on her toes, so to speak.

"Walk on tiptoe for three steps, go to the sink and fill two glasses of water, hum 'Old MacDonald Had a Farm.'"

"Shake your head five times, count to ten in a whisper, say 'my cat has whiskers' three times as fast as you can."

"Walk to the table, put three fingers on the table, draw a red flower."

Sometimes Gail needed a break from jumping, hopping, shak-ing, and waving. That's when I listed numbers and words for her to remember.

"Repeat these numbers: *13, 36, 98, 89.*"

"Repeat these words: *cat, mouse, telephone, flower, run.*"

"Repeat these words: *big balloon, yellow turtle, five scissors, fast runners.*"

You already know, I'm sure, that children love bossing adults around. Sometimes in playing DO THIS, DO THAT, I let Gail boss me around. You should let your child boss you from time to time.

"Daddy, when I say go, you have to growl like a bear, make a funny face, and pretend you're an elephant. . . . GO!"

"Grrrrr . . ."

TALK A DRAWING

MATERIALS

blank paper
two boxes of crayons
optional: masking tape

*T*ALK A DRAWING is a variation of DO THIS, DO THAT. Instead of telling your child to clap or walk on tiptoe, have him draw circles and stars. Actually, TALK A DRAWING is an excellent game to play with more than one child. It's a bit difficult for younger children, but older children enjoy it and benefit, too.

You and your child (or children) should each take a few sheets of paper and a box of crayons and sit where you can hear each other but can't see each other's drawings. Once you're set up, start telling your child (or children) what to draw. For example: "Draw a blue square in the center of the page." Both you and the child draw a blue square in the center of your respective pages. Now give a second instruction, afterward a third, and so on. As you play, you'll need to clarify certain instructions. When I play,

to draw a square means to draw the outline: ☐ . To color a

square means to fill in the shape with color: ▨ . If children

get confused or can't remember instructions, don't hesitate to explain or repeat yourself. Once each paper is filled with shapes and lines, compare drawings. Every drawing gives a visual picture of how accurately a child follows directions.

Here is a talked drawing I once gave Gail. Sometimes I gave separate instructions; sometimes I grouped instructions together. The first instruction was to draw a blue circle in the center of the page.

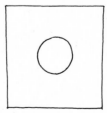

Her next job was to color the circle red.

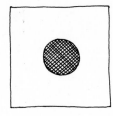

Then she had to draw an orange square in the upper right-hand corner of the page, and a green triangle in the upper left-hand corner of the page.

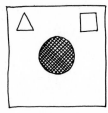

(If your child has trouble telling left from right, label the back of his hands with a small piece of masking tape.)

Next came a blue circle in the left bottom corner and another one on the right. The blue circles had to be filled in with yellow.

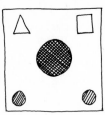

Finally she had to draw a wavy green line from the triangle to the center circle and a straight purple line from the square to the center circle.

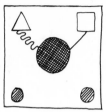

Instructions finished, we compared drawings.

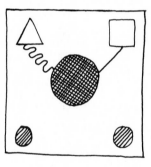 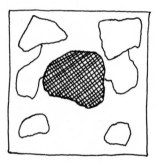

My drawing   Gail's drawing

There were obvious differences. I showed Gail how some of these resulted from her difficulty in following directions. She had two wavy lines instead of one wavy line and one straight line, and she'd forgotten to color the bottom circles yellow. Other discrepancies were due to individual drawing styles: her square and triangle were larger than mine, her wavy line waved less formally, and her circles weren't exactly circular. I assured Gail that drawing variations aren't always mistakes. We agreed that she'd followed directions fairly well. Still, we felt her next attempt would be even better. So we took out crayons, returned to our drawing corners, and started to work.

Have you ever tried talking to someone and listening to them at the same time? You talk, and you hear sounds, but you don't understand what you hear. This surprises most children. They are sure they can talk and listen simultaneously. Proving them wrong makes a good game and a good listening exercise.

For HARD LISTENING to work, both players must talk continuously. If your child stops talking, even for one second, he'll start to listen. To keep your child yakking away, help him decide what to talk about before the game begins. He might describe an exciting event such as a birthday party, a fight with a younger brother, or a trip to the circus. He could recount the plot of a TV show or movie. He could also describe how to feed the cat, how to play baseball, or how to make a valentine card. You have to pick your own topic, too. Your child might have an idea about this.

Once you both have topics in mind, start the game. Count "one, two, three, GO"—and burst into talk. The outburst needn't last long. Thirty seconds, more or less, will do. As soon as the talk-talk-talk wears thin, call "STOP." Now your child tries to tell what he heard. Most children are struck by how little this turns out to be. They may pick up a word or two, but they don't hear much more than that. After your child tells what he's heard, he will undoubtedly want to know what you heard, or better yet, what you didn't hear.

If your child is excited about the game, play again. But don't play HARD LISTENING more than two or three times on a single occasion. The game is fun, but only in small doses. Instead do a little HARD LISTENING today, continue the game tomorrow, and then try again next week. Every time you play, your child will try to listen a bit more intensely than normal conversation demands. This intense listening is very good for him. With HARD LISTENING, you can take a spare half minute and transform it into an instant listening lesson.

WRONG-SPEED CONVER-SATIONS

Has your child ever deliberately put a 45 RPM record on the record player at 33⅓ RPM? It sounds funny because the words are s-t-r-e-t-c-h-e-d o-u-t. How about playing a 45 RPM record at 78 RPM? This time it sounds funny because the words are *speeded up.*

WRONG-SPEED CONVERSATIONS consist of stretching out or speeding up conversations with your child. These conversations are most fun when introduced as part of your daily routine.

"G-e-t y-o-u-r h-a-t a-n-d c-o-a-t. W-e'-r-e g-o-i-n-g o-u-t-s-i-d-e."

"Mom, why are you talking so funny?"

"It's a new game. I talk at the wrong speed and you try to understand me. If you don't understand something I say, I'll try it again. I m-i-g-h-t- t-a-l-k t-o-o s-l-o-w, or [in a high, way-too-fast voice] I-might-talk-too-fast. You-can-answer-me-at-the-wrong-speed. N-o-w d-o-n'-t f-o-r-g-e-t y-o-u-r g-l-o-v-e-s. I-t i-s c-o-l-d o-u-t."

There is a good educational reason for talking in slow motion. When children sound out words, they have to hear two different things. They must hear and recognize the sounds of individual letters, and they must condense these sounds into a single word. This isn't so easy. Children tend to concentrate so hard on individual letter sounds that they fail to integrate the sounds into a word. They hear the *b* sound, the *a* sound, and the *t* sound, but can't bring these sounds together into *bat.* Talking in slow motion helps children hear separate sounds as a single word.

The reason for talking in speeded-up motion is that it makes the game even sillier and more fun.

*T*here are two reasons why rhyming helps a beginning reader. First, rhyming develops a child's sensitivity to sounds. Second, a child who hears the relationship between *hop, pop,* and *stop* should find it easy to read words that fit the same sound and visual pattern—*flop, mop,* and *top,* for instance.

You can't assume your child will learn to rhyme on his own. Although I have known three-year-olds who rhyme like poets, I've also known perfectly intelligent eight-year-olds who can't rhyme at all.

Carla was an eight-year-old who couldn't rhyme, but the following games helped her quite a lot. The first is a finish-the-rhyme game. I began a rhyming phrase, but left out the final rhyming word. Carla finished the phrase by adding this word. Any rhyming word that makes sense is a good answer. For example:

My old gray cat,
caught a great big ————.
(*Rat, bat, hat,* or *gnat* will do.)

Here are some more phrases:

I will pick a flower,
and be back in one ————.

Learning to read a book
proves I'm as smart as I ————.

This is a star,
it shines near and ————.

I like to run and hop,
I go until I ————.

It is fun to rhyme,
I can do it any ————.

If you're like me, you'll enjoy inventing these little jingles. If you're not like me, try this second rhyming game with your child instead.

In the second game, the two (or three, or four) players make a rhyming chain. A rhyming chain is a series of rhyming words generated one at a time by consecutive players. When a player runs out of words, the chain is broken. Here is a chain Carla and I made.

I said, "Jump."

She said, "Bump."

I said, "Lump."

She said, "Stump."

I said, "Hump."

She said, "Thumb."

"Wait a second, Carla. Listen to this and tell me which word doesn't fit: jump, bump, hump, thumb." Carla heard her mistake. She tried to think of a new word to add to the chain.

She said, "Cump."

"Well, that rhymes, but it isn't a word. Give it one more try." Carla couldn't think of a rhyming word. The chain was broken. We started a new chain.

"Dance" said Carla.

"Prance" said I.

So, when you have some idle time,
teach your child how to rhyme.

One day I was walking with a friend. We saw two girls jumping rope and chanting:

> John and Mary sitting in a tree,
> K*I*S*S*I*N*G
> First comes love,
> Then comes marriage,
> Then comes Mary with a baby carriage.

I turned to my friend and commented, "You see those girls over there? They're not just jumping rope. They're helping themselves become better readers."

My friend looked skeptical. I explained that learning chants demands concentration, memorization, sensitivity to sounds, rhyme, and rhythm. Each of these skills is of enormous value to beginning readers (as well as to advanced readers, nuclear physicists, orchestral conductors, and so on). By chanting as they jumped rope, the two girls were sharpening their skills.

What's true of jump-rope chants is also true of other word games: for instance, tongue twisters, rhymes, and riddles. Children almost always love to learn and memorize such chants, riddles, twists, or rhymes. Because they are enthusiastic about this memorization, all you need to do is pick out one and offer to help your child learn it.

Sometimes a riddle or tongue twister will be so short that hearing it once or twice is all a child needs in order to remember it. For instance, here is a riddle that is easy enough to learn:

Question: How do you know if an elephant is in bed with you?
Answer: You smell the peanuts on his breath.

Most chants, rhymes, and tongue twisters require more practice. Don't feel a chant has to be taught in one day. It's probably better to work a bit one day and a bit more the next, until your child has the chant down pat.

You can teach your child the chants, riddles, tongue twisters, and rhymes you recall from your own childhood. You can also learn new ones together. A library or bookstore with a good selection of children's books is a sensible place to find new material. Here are some personal favorites.

JUMP-ROPE CHANTS

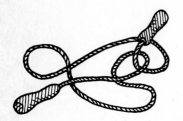

I like coffee, I like tea;
I like the boys [girls], and the boys [girls] like me.

Teddy bear, teddy bear, turn around.
Teddy bear, teddy bear, touch the ground.
Teddy bear, teddy bear, touch your shoe.
Teddy bear, teddy bear, I love you.
Teddy bear, teddy bear, turn off the light.
Teddy bear, teddy bear, say good night.

Postman, postman do your duty;
send this letter to an American beauty.
Don't you stop, and don't delay;
get it to her right away.

RHYMES

I eat my peas with honey;
I've done it all my life.
It makes the peas taste funny;
but it keeps them on my knife.

When you get married and have twins,
don't come to me for safety pins.

One bright day in the middle of the night,
two blind men went out to fight.
Back to back they faced each other,
pulled out their knives and shot each other.
A deaf policeman heard their cry,
and that's the truth, I wouldn't lie.

Mabel, Mabel, if you're able,
get your elbows off the table.
This is not a horse's stable!

TONGUE TWISTERS

(Say each one three times as fast as you can.)

Fruit float

She sells seashells by the seashore.

If two witches were watching two watches, which witch would watch which watch?

RIDDLES

Question: What do you call the school hamster?
Answer: A teacher's pet.

Question: What gets wet when it's drying?
Answer: A towel.

Question: What has six eyes but can't see?
Answer: Three blind mice.

Question: What does the ground say during a rainstorm?
Answer: If this keeps up, my name is mud.

Question: What has teeth but can't bite?
Answer: A comb.

Keep your ears open when you're at the playground. You may hear something new.

chapter 5.

Letter Sounds

How do you spell "fish"? George Bernard Shaw spelled it "ghoti." He took the *gh* from *enough*, *o* from *women*, *ti* from *nation*, and put them together: *ghoti.* Yes, it's hard to learn to spell, and almost as hard to learn to read. Letters in the English language make all kinds of unpredictable sounds. Children spend three years, sometimes more, learning these sounds. They start with consonant sounds, for instance, the sound *b* makes. Then they must learn to pick out the *b*-sound in words like *bat* or *cab.* Later they learn vowel sounds. Again they must recognize sounds in isolation and also identify them in words. Slowly they master the standard combinations, as when *kn* makes the *n*-sound, and the nonstandard combinations, as when *gh* makes the *f*-sound. Learning these things is a lot of work, and children need all the help they can get.

The games in this chapter are designed to make letter sounds easier, or at least fun, to learn. One of the games combines jelly beans with learning letter sounds. In another, you'll play a traditional children's game, GRANDMOTHER'S TRUNK, adapted to teach letter sounds. There is a game for making up silly sentences and a board game complete with spinner. Pick out the games you like; ignore the rest.

You might want to alternate the games in this chapter with the games in Chapter Three. In fact, it's a good idea to do so. The two chapters together give a rounded approach to learning the sounds of letters.

*I*t hadn't been easy to teach Barbara consonant sounds. I tried this, I tried that, but not until we started making a CONSONANT BOX did good things begin to happen.

A CONSONANT BOX is merely a file box filled with index cards and alphabet dividers. Put in all the consonants and leave out the vowels *a, e, i, o, u* (vowels require other games). The idea of the CONSONANT BOX is to write words for every consonant and file them under the appropriate letter.

Barbara was delighted to have the box because it seemed a nice, grown-up object. When I explained that the box would help her remember letter sounds, she was wary but agreeable.

"Since your name is Barbara, let's start filling your box with *b* words. Do you know the sound *b* makes?"

Yes, she did. I told her to think of words that begin with *b*. She had trouble doing this; she knew the *b*-sound in isolation, but couldn't connect it with words. I made suggestions. Then she thought of a few words, too. Together we listed a dozen or so, and then I asked her to pick her five favorite *b* words. Barbara picked *balloon, blizzard, blink, butterfly,* and *baseball.* I wrote these words on individual file cards. We decorated the cards with colorful illustrations. Neither of us could think of a good illustration for *blizzard* so we left that card blank, except for the word.

MATERIALS

file box
index cards
alphabet dividers
pen
coloring materials
optional: oak tag or
poster board
glue
scissors
magazines
transparent tape

We filed these beautiful cards in the CONSONANT BOX under *b*.

Having filed cards for *b*, Barbara was ready to start a new letter. We began to think of *l*-words—*laugh, lizard, licorice* . . .

Some letters make more than one sound. The CONSONANT BOX can help your child learn two sounds for *c* (*c* as in *cat* and *cent*), two sounds for *g* (as in *giant* and *good*), and two sounds for *x* (as in *xylophone* and *x-ray*).

Filling in the sections of the card file letter by letter is one way to go about playing with the CONSONANT BOX. There are other ways, too. One day Barbara and I were talking about animals. It turned out that she had a lot to say about all sorts of beasts. After the discussion I asked her to name three animals she'd like to own, and she responded with koala bear, monkey, and puppy. We talked about the first-letter sound of each animal. "*Monkey*, that begins 'mmm,' 'mmmm.' That's the sound *m* makes. *Monkey* begins with the letter *m*. Let's see, what's the first letter in *puppy*?" Once the first letters were determined, I wrote index cards for each animal and we drew matching pictures. Then we filed the animal cards in the box. On another day, we talked about monsters. Barbara found out that *vampire* begins with *v*, *werewolf* begins with *w*, and *ghost* begins with *g*. These monsters were carefully imprisoned in the CONSONANT BOX. Your child might collect foods, cars, angry words, colors, or pretty things in his CONSONANT BOX.

One day I had a pile of magazines waiting for Barbara. We leafed through them, looking for interesting pictures. Barbara found several she liked. When a picture was small enough, we cut it out, pasted it on an index card, labeled the card, and added it to the box. Sometimes we used a small part of a larger picture.

"Look at this fashion model. She has a very red mouth. Do you want to cut out her mouth and add it to the box?"

The mouth went into the box under *m*.

Occasionally we looked through a children's dictionary. There were plenty of good CONSONANT BOX words there.

"This word says *goldfish*. Would you like to add *goldfish* to your *g* words?"

Once your child's box has a number of cards, you might enjoy playing some games with them. Here are a few games Barbara and I liked. In one, the object was for Barbara to identify the first letter of various words. I took a handful of cards from the box and read the words one by one. If she knew the first letter, she got one point. If she didn't know, I told her. We went through cards until she accumulated fifteen points and won the game.

We also played a guessing game. I picked a card from the box. Barbara tried to guess what card I'd picked. I gave her hints: "It's an animal that begins with the letter *d*" (*dog*). "It's bigger than a jungle gym, has leaves, and begins with the letter *t*" (*tree*).

Sometimes we simply looked through Barbara's cards and discussed koala bears, balloons, or vampires. What impressed me was how Barbara used her box when I wasn't around. She showed the cards to friends. She studied them quietly on her own. Not all children enjoy CONSONANT BOXES as much as Barbara did. Some children find putting cards in a file box more of a chore than a game. They'll make the effort for a letter or two and then they'll moan, "Do we have to do this any more?" The answer to such a complaint is, "No, let's do something else." An abandoned CONSONANT BOX can always be used to store recipes. For children like Barbara, however, this little box is one of the soundest sound investments you can make.

WHERE'S THE SOUND?

MATERIALS

three paper cups

jelly beans, peanuts, raisins, or some other favorite small snack

paper

pen

Where's the *p*-sound in *pillow*? Is it at the beginning, middle, or end of the word? Where's the *p*-sound in *capital*? Where's the *p*-sound in *soap*? Where's the *s*-sound in *swim*? Where's the *s*-sound in *whisper*? Where's the *s*-sound in *boss*?

I asked Mickey these questions. The right answer demanded a great deal of knowledge. Mickey had to know the *s*-sound and the *p*-sound and he also had to identify these sounds within words. Asking and answering such questions is a game in itself, but Mickey preferred a sweeter version.

I took three paper cups. One cup was labeled "beginning," one was labeled "middle," and the third was labeled "end." I put these cups on a table next to a small bowl of jelly beans.

Then the questions started. Where's the *d*-sound in *detective*? Instead of telling me, Mickey dropped a jelly bean in one of the three cups. If he picked the correct cup, in this case the beginning cup, he won. Winning meant he got to eat the jelly bean. Some questions let Mickey eat more than one jelly bean at a time. Where's the *t*-sound in *taste*? If Mickey listened carefully, he'd get two jelly beans, one for the beginning, one for the end. (The sound and not the spelling is what counts in this game; *t* is the last sound in *taste*, although not the last letter.) When you play, make sure that you pronounce the words clearly. You might ask your child to repeat each word before he commits his jelly bean to a cup.

Start raising your child's blood sugar with questions like these:

Where's the *l*-sound in *silly*?
Where's the *b*-sound in *block*?
Where's the *o*-sound in *radio*?
Where's the *v*-sound in *television*?
Where's the *p*-sound in *surprise*?
Where's the *n*-sound in *kitchen*?
Where's the *s*-sound in *sneakers*?
Where's the *t*-sound in *spaghetti*?
Where's the *m*-sound in *mayonnaise*?
Where's the *t*-sound in *elephant*?
Where's the *l*-sound in *lilacs*?
Where's the *s*-sound in *seasons*?

PURPLE PENGUINS PICK PINE- APPLES

OPTIONAL
MATERIALS

paper
pencil

When you see the letter *b*, you associate it with the *b*-as-in-*boy* sound. You associate the letter *p* with the *p*-as-in-*pink* sound. It's easy for you to hear the difference between *b* and *p* because you've done it so many times. Your child, lacking your listening experience, may have trouble distinguishing these sounds. Yet he must learn them accurately in order to read. PURPLE PENGUINS PICK PINEAPPLES can give him practice.

In a true PURPLE PENGUINS PICK PINEAPPLES sentence, every word begins with the same sound. In a false PURPLE PENGUINS sentence, one or more words begin with a different sound. Here are examples.

> A true PURPLE PENGUIN sentence: *Take two tangerines to Texas.*
> Another true PURPLE PENGUIN sentence: *Kangaroos can't catch kittens.* (It's the sounds, not the letters, that must be identical.)
> A false PURPLE PENGUIN sentence: *Busy Bobby buys pickles.*

To play the game, make up both true and false sentences. Your child listens to one sentence at a time. He tries to tell true sentences from false ones. It's a good idea to have him say the sentence out loud; this helps children differentiate sounds. After a sentence is identified as false, the child must tell which word is the mismatch. When your child figures out a PURPLE PENGUIN sentence correctly, let him know how proud of him you are.

Here are a variety of PURPLE PENGUIN sentences, both true and false, to start the game rolling.

> Lucky Lynn licks lemons.
> Burton buys blue boxes.
> Sally keeps sandwiches safe.
> Happy Harry has hair.
> Marvelous Mike needs many marionettes.
> Quiet queens eat quail.
> Fifty foresters visit Florida.

Pretty princes pick petunias.
Pat bought pink pears.
Good camels get going.
Charlie's chicken shivers.
Smiling Sam sometimes sneaks spaghetti.
Yesterday yaks yowled.
Donald doesn't doodle.
Elephants entertain angry enemies.
Antelope antlers catch ants.
Sylvia zippers suitcases. (This is tricky—z in *zipper* is
    not the same sound as s in *suitcases*.)
Roving Robert races red reindeer.
Otters always occupy Ossining. (This is tricky, too.)

There's a variation on this game for older children. You and your child construct as long a PURPLE PENGUIN sentence, or even a PURPLE PENGUIN story, as you can. Help each other think of good words to make the story grow.

"Let's see, we have 'Bossy Betsy.' Now what could bossy Betsy do? She could brag . . . bother . . . beat . . . what do you think?"

It may be necessary for long sentences and stories to include words that don't fit the sound pattern. That's OK; just try to keep odd words to a minimum. As you construct the story, write it down. Using s, I began this story: *Sensible Sally sails a sailboat slowly. Sally sips sweet sassafras soda sitting by the sails. Since Sally sails so slowly, she sees seven strange sycamore trees swaying softly by the shore . . . .* Once the story is completed, say it all together, aloud. You might have a terrific tongue twister.

GRAND-
MOTHER'S
TRUNK

GRANDMOTHER'S TRUNK can be played with two, three, five, even ten people. It is especially popular on car rides or at birthday parties.

Player One: In my grandmother's trunk, I packed a watermelon.
Player Two: In my grandmother's trunk, I packed a watermelon and a pot of tea.
Player Three: In my grandmother's trunk, I packed a watermelon, a pot of tea, and a spider's web.
Player Four: In my grandmother's trunk, I packed a watermelon, a pot of tea, a spider's web, and a pair of shoes.

You may recognize this game; generations of children have played it. Each player must list everything already contained in grandmother's trunk, then add one item more. The list must be in proper order: watermelon first, pot of tea next, spider's web third, and so on. If you forget something or get the order wrong, you're out of the game.

This traditional version of GRANDMOTHER'S TRUNK is a fine listening game. It helps your child remember the things he hears. By modifying the game a bit, you can also help your child learn letter sounds.

Once your child understands how to play, tell him that grandmother has become very picky. She will only allow things in her trunk that begin with the sound *b* makes. Make sure he understands the *b*-sound, and then start the game. "In my grandmother's trunk, I packed some *b*ubble gum . . . a *b*aseball . . . a *b*at . . . a *b*ottle of vinegar . . ."

Each time you play, indulge grandmother in a new packing preference. Grandmother might insist on things beginning with the sound *p* makes: "In my grandmother's trunk, I packed a *p*ancake . . . a *p*encil . . . a *p*anda . . ." Grandmother might make the game even more challenging and require that everything begin with the sound *sh* makes: "In my grandmother's trunk, I packed *sh*aving cream . . . a *sh*rimp cocktail . . . a *sh*ell . . ." And while she's being difficult, she could demand that everything begin with a particular vowel sound, for instance short *e* (as in *egg*): "In my grandmother's trunk, I packed an *e*lephant . . . an *e*gg roll . . . an *E*skimo . . ."

When your child is good at beginning sounds, grandmother can decide to accept only things that end with the same sound, for instance, a *t*-sound. In that case, grandmother's trunk would carry a ca*t*, a baseball ba*t*, and a ska*t*e. (The sound, not the spelling, is what counts in GRANDMOTHER'S TRUNK. First things first.)

When grandmother is particular, there are two ways to lose the game—a player might forget the items previously packed or might have trouble adding an object that meets grandmother's packing prerequisites. In either case, the game's over. So dump out the trunk and see if you want to start packing again.

ALPHABET WORDS

MATERIALS

pen and paper

I learned this game from a friend who remembered playing it after dinner with his sister. The smile on his face as he recalled the game convinced me that I should give it a try with my students. Sure enough, it was a big success, not with all, but certainly with many children.

```
A        N
B        O
C        P
D        Q
E        R
F        S
G        T
H        U
I        V
J        W
K        X
L        Y
M        Z
```

This is an ALPHABET WORDS playing board. It's just a piece of paper with the alphabet written on it. The goal of the game is to fill the board with twenty-six words. Each word should begin with a different letter—*acorn* for *A*, *bubble gum* for *B*, and so on.

Let your child come up with as many of the words as he can. You can give hints. "I'm thinking of a furry little animal that begins with *H*." If hints don't work, give him the word. "I was thinking of *hamster*. The next time we pass a pet store, let's go in and look at the hamsters." When either you or your child think of an alphabet word, write it down on the playing board. If your child wants to write the word, that's even better. You don't have to follow alphabetical order, although it might be fun to try. Here is a completed game board.

Acorn	Noodle
Bubble gum	Octopus
Caterpillar	Purple
Diamond	Quiet
Eggs	Roses
Farm	Strawberries
Garbage	Turtle
Hamster	Unicorn
Ice	Violet
Jelly	Witch
Kangaroo	X-ray
Lunch	Yesterday
Mom	Zoom

It can be fun to give ALPHABET WORDS a theme. Try thinking of twenty-six foods, one for every letter of the alphabet. After foods, try coming up with twenty-six animals, names of games, jobs, places to live, or ways of feeling. Make an effort to fill in the entire alphabet; you can use a dictionary. Since, even with effort, it's unlikely you'll come up with a food that begins with U or an animal that begins with X (there's no such thing as a Xebra), just leave those letters blank. If only half the alphabet is filled, the game is still valuable. ALPHABET WORDS gets your child thinking about letter sounds. "An animal that begins with *V*? V-v-v . . ." is as important a part of learning letter sounds as the final victory— "*Vulture!*"

LINKING WORDS

LINKING WORDS is a good game to play while you're doing household chores. For example, you can play while you and your child clear the table or pick up toys.

cat-tip-pink-keep-pear-rain-napkin-needle

These are linking words: each word begins with the last sound of the previous word. *Cat* links with *tip*, *pear* links with *rain*, *needle* links with *love*. Why does *needle* link with *love*? Because the *l*-sound is the last sound in *needle*, even if not the last letter. This game is about sounds. That's also why *love* links with *violet*. When you play LINKING WORDS, let your child pick a starting word, then take turns linking on new words. If your child makes a mistake, let him try a new word. If he has trouble hearing the last sound of a word exaggerate—*cat-t-t-t.* The game ends when one of you runs out of words and/or patience.

That's all there is to it, yet LINKING WORDS demands sophisticated understanding of letter sounds. First your child hears a word. Then he must isolate the last sound in that word: it has to be so firm in his mind that he can use it to generate a new word, a word where this same sound comes first instead of last. This may seem fairly tame to you, but it's not for a child who is just beginning to master letter sounds.

*T*his game takes a certain amount of time to prepare, but I promise, the work pays off.

CHICKENS AND WHALES is a who-can-get-to-the-finish-first board game. It helps teach children the sounds *sh, th, ch,* and *wh* —sounds that are particularly difficult for children to master. Players move along the board by spinning a spinner (children invariably love spinners).

MATERIALS

oak tag or poster board
paper fastener
scissors
glue
pen
a game token for each player
(a token might be a penny,
a paper clip, a button, or
any tiny object)

To make the spinner, start with a square piece of oak tag approximately 6" x 6" for the base. Draw a circle in the square, and divide the circle into quarters. Write letters inside the circle as in the illustration:

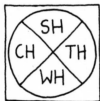

Now you need an arrow to spin. Cut one out of oak tag.

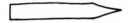

Push a paper fastener through the center of the arrow.

Then push the fastener through the center of the spinner. Press the fastener tails down, and spin the arrow.

front   back

Sometimes the arrow gets stuck. If this happens, wiggle it around a little. This will widen the hole, and you'll be able to spin again.

Now for the playing board. It looks something like this:

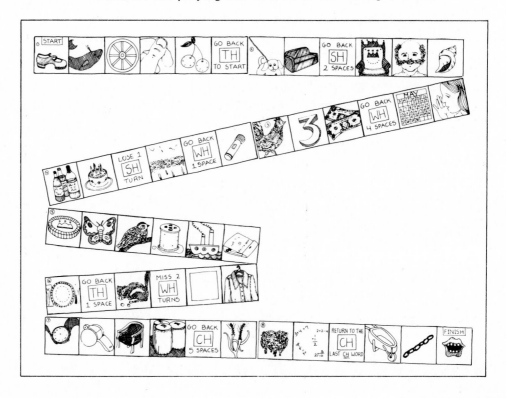

This is quite easy to make; I've practically done it for you. At the end of this game description are eight strips of squares already drawn. You can photocopy this illustration, cut out the strips from the copy, and paste them on the board (an 11" x 14" piece of oak tag makes a fine board). Of course, if you'd prefer designing your own board, using cutouts from magazines or your original drawings, go right ahead.

Here's how the board works. Every picture square has a drawing of something which is spelled with *sh, th, ch,* or *wh*. (See page 106 for key to drawings.) Each player spins the spinner. After spinning, you move your playing token to the next square that has a picture of something with the right letter combination. If the spinner goes to *ch*, you must move to the picture of the chicken, the chair, or the watch, whichever comes first. Then the next person spins. Not all squares have drawings. Some say "lose your turn," or "go back two spaces." Naturally, you must obey. This makes the game exciting.

There's another rule. As you move your token around, you must say the name of each picture you pass and state which letter combination is involved. When you go backwards, you have to do the same thing.

Here is the beginning of the game that I played with Jason. This picture shows the first few playing squares.

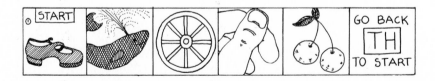

Jason went first. He gave the arrow a powerful twirl. It stopped spinning on *th*. Jason moved his token past *shoe*, past *whale*, past *wheel*, and stopped at *thumb*. As he moved his piece, he identified the relevant sound for each picture: "Shoe-*sh*, whale-*wh*, wheel-*wh*, thumb-*th*." If Jason couldn't identify a picture or was perplexed about a sound, I cleared up his confusion. After Jason landed on *thumb*, it was my turn to spin. The arrow spun to *wh*. While moving, I said the sounds for each picture: "Shoe-*sh*, whale-*wh*." I went only two squares in this turn. "That's not so hot," I said, but wasn't really disturbed. In CHICKENS AND WHALES, you may be behind one minute and spin ahead the next. Conversely, you may be way ahead but land on a penalty square and have to move backwards. This keeps the suspense alive from the first chicken to the last whale.

Incidentally, this is a good game for playing with two, three, or four children.

KEY TO DRAWINGS:

row 1: shoe, whale, wheel, thumb, cherry, penalty square
row 2: leash, couch, penalty square, throne, whiskers, shell
row 3: chicken, three, cash, penalty square, month, whisper
row 4: whiskey, birthday, penalty square, beach, penalty square, flashlight
row 5: checker, moth, whippoorwill, thread, ship, matches
row 6: dish, penalty square, chipmunk, penalty square, white, shirt
row 7: watch, whistle, chair, trash, penalty square, wheat
row 8: sheep, math, penalty square, wheelbarrow, chain, mouth

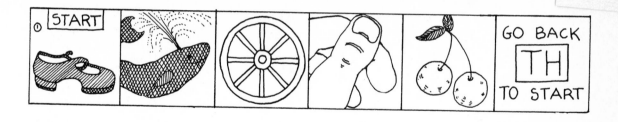

⑤

⑦ GO BACK CH 5 SPACES

⑥ GO BACK TH 1 SPACE | MISS 2 WH TURNS

⑧ 3+4=7 2+2=4 $\frac{+1}{2}$ 8-6=2 $2\overline{)10}^{5}$ | RETURN TO THE CH LAST CH WORD | FINISH

chapter 6.

Super Sounds Games

Here are four games for learning the sounds of letters—games to help your child remember that *b* makes a sound as in *boy* and *d* a sound as in *dog.* One of the games involves jumping around, another involves throwing things, one uses cards and another uses checkers. There's a game for every temperament and mood.

Each game can be played at five levels of difficulty, as you'll see in the instructions. I've provided sample games at each level. Suppose you want to make up games of your own using these different levels of difficulty? All you have to do is turn to the appendix, "A List of Important Sounds." There you will find the five levels laid out in detail.

Most children learn the sounds in levels one and two during first grade, level three in second grade, and the last levels in third grade. Your child may go through these levels more quickly or slowly—it doesn't matter. The important thing is that your child enjoy his time with these games. Don't feel in any rush to get to level three, or four, or five. When a game is too hard, it loses appeal. If your child forgets many letter sounds, declares he is bored, or complains it's not fun any more—then stop playing. Next time, play with easier sounds. Making the games easier almost always makes them more fun.

RABBIT SOUNDS

How can you help a jumpy child learn letter sounds? Play a jumpy learning game. RABBIT SOUNDS is one of the jumpiest games I know, very useful with a fidgety child like Dori. The game is like hopscotch and it let Dori learn and move simultaneously.

You can play RABBIT SOUNDS on any hard floor or outside pavement. Using chalk or masking tape, design a playing board. Make the board large enough so that your child has to work a bit at jumping from square to square. Keep hopscotch-size boards in mind. Each playing square should have a letter written in its center.

When you're ready to play, tell your child which lettered square to jump to. But don't name the letter. Instead say something like, "Jump to the first sound in *donkey*." Or "Jump to the last sound in *friend*." Or "Jump to the square that sounds like *duh*." You can also ask the child what sounds a letter makes. When he gives the right answer, he can jump to that square. (Coming up with these questions is your own equivalent of jumping around.)

I played with Dori on the board shown above. Here are some of the instructions I gave:

"Jump to the first sound in the word *vitamin*."

"Jump to the *puh*-sounding letter."

"If you can tell me the sound *n* makes, you can jump there."

"Jump to the last sound in *dragon*."

110

"Jump to the letter that makes the *juh*-sound." (On this board only *g* makes the *juh*-sound; on another board, Dori might have had to choose between jumping to *g* or to *j*.)

"Jump to the first letter sound in the word *go*." (Dori had to jump in place because *g*, the *juh*-sound, is also the first sound in *go*.)

"You can jump to *c* if you can tell me the two sounds *c* makes."

If Dori didn't know the two sounds of *c*, or the first sound in *go*, I told her. Then she made her leap. When Dori's legs were tired out, the game was over.

Dori was happy to play RABBIT SOUNDS almost every single day. She'd never had such an active reading lesson before, and she took to it like a rabbit to carrots. For several weeks we played with consonants. Soon Dori had learned consonants so well that I added vowel jumps to the game.

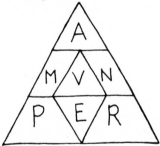

"Jump to the letter that makes *ee*."
"Jump to the first letter in *astronaut*."
"Jump to the first letter in *egg*."
"Jump to the last sound in the word *heffalump*."

Once your child conquers consonants and vowels, he can start jumping to harder sounds. Here are boards at five levels of difficulty.

Level One

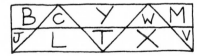

Level Two

Level Three

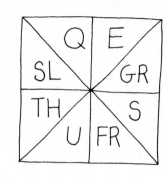

Level Four

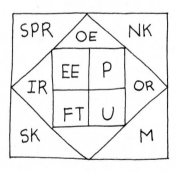

Level Five

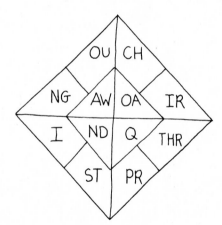

You can devise boards of your own by picking letters from the "List of Important Sounds" at the back of this book.

*T*hese letter cards are used to play OOPS.

OOPS

MATERIALS

index cards

pen

Although Pedro hated almost every other sound-teaching game, he liked OOPS. Pedro and I played OOPS a lot.

I piled the letter cards in a deck. Pedro picked the top card and tried to read the letter sound—not the name of the letter, but the sound it makes. If he knew the sound, fine. If he didn't, his troubles began. With each mistake, Pedro was awarded one of the letters in the word *oops.* His first mistake brought him an *o.* His second mistake brought a second *o.* His third mistake earned him a *p.* For his fourth mistake, he got *s. O-o-p-s!* Pedro lost the game. On the other hand, if he went through the entire deck making fewer than four mistakes, he won.

Whenever Pedro made an error, I'd tell him the correct sound. This way he slowly caught on. When he could go through a whole deck without an *oops,* it was time for a new set of cards.

There should be about fifteen to twenty letter cards in a set. You can make the letter cards out of index cards, or perhaps index cards cut in half. Here are five OOPS decks at different levels of difficulty. Needless to say, start your child at the simplest level and work your way up from there.

Level One

b, c (as in *cat* and *cent*), f, g (as in *go* and *giant*), j, k, l, m, n, p, q, r, s, t, v, w, x (as in *xylophone* and *ax*), y (as in *yarn*), z.

Level Two

a (as in *at* and *ate*), b, c, d, e (as in *egg* and *eat*) g, h, i (as in *it* and *ice*), j, k, l, o (as in *otter* and *oat*), q, u (as in *us* and *use*), v, x, z, er, ir, or.

Level Three

a, c, f, i, o, p, v, x, y (as in *yarn, my,* and *silly*), ar, ur, bl, cl, gr, pl, sn, sm, sp, tr, ch, th, wh, sh.

Level Four

i, e, v, x, y, z, or, er, ar, tw, sc, cr, dr, sw, spl, str, nd, ng, oa, ea, ue, sh, th.

Level Five

a, g, j, o, u, q, or, ur, fl, fr, sk, sl, sn, thr, nd, ft, ai, ch, ee, aw, ew, ow (as in *cow* and *blow*), ou (as in *out* and *trouble*), oy, oo (as in *boot* and *foot*).

At the back of this book you'll find the appendix "A List of Important Sounds." Use it to draw up OOPS decks of your own.

*I*f you'd walked into my work-room while I was helping Marsha learn letter sounds, you'd have seen the two of us sitting on the floor throwing pennies and paper clips at a muffin tin. Marsha was trying to land six pennies, one in each muffin cup, before I could land six paper clips in the same cups. We took turns throwing. First Marsha threw a penny, then I threw a paper clip, then Marsha threw a penny, and so on. Inside each muffin cup was a small slip of paper on which I'd written a letter.

MATERIALS

a six-cup muffin tin
(or an egg carton cut in half)
small items for tossing
(such as paper clips, pennies,
and dried beans)
paper
scissors
pencil

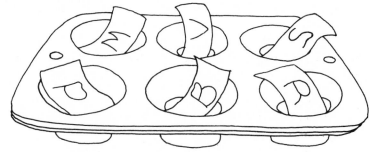

Whenever one of Marsha's pennies landed in a cup, she had to tell me that cup's letter sound. If she knew the sound, her penny stayed there.

"Good toss, Marsha," I'd say when she aced a throw. "Can you tell me the sound that *p* makes?"

"*Puh.*"

"Terrific, your penny can stay right there." If she didn't know the sound, I told it to her; but she had to remove the penny. When one of my paper clips landed in a cup, it was my turn to say that letter sound.

"That's *c*. *C* makes two sounds. It makes *kah* in *cat* and *sss* in *cent*."

Obviously I had a big advantage over Marsha: I know my letter sounds. We compensated for this by making it harder for me to land paper clips—Marsha perched close to the muffin tin, while I sat farther away. That evened things up a bit. But since I was still winning more than my share of games, we increased my handicap. I threw the paper clips with my left hand, which made us equal competitors.

If you don't have a muffin tin lying around, you can use an egg carton with the lid cut off. Egg holders are small, unfortunately, which makes it hard to land paper clips and pennies. On the other hand, with an egg carton you can expand the game. At first cut the carton in half, so that you and your child play with six egg holders. Another day, take a new carton and cut it so that eight or ten egg holders can be used. If your child has excellent aim and will soon be trying out for the 76ers, don't cut the carton at all. Leave it whole and try filling the entire dozen.

When Marsha first started SOUND TOSS, we played with easy sounds. Each time Marsha won a game, I refilled the tin—using some old and some new sounds, and gradually introducing more difficult letters. Sometimes I let the sounds get too hard too quickly, and then the game turned into work instead of play. I'd get things back on the track by stopping the game long enough to place easier sounds in the muffin tin. Here are five sets of letters for SOUND TOSS:

A **level-one** muffin tin might use these letters: b, x (as in *xylophone* and *ax*), p, j, r, t.

A **level-two** muffin tin might contain these letters: e (as in *egg* and *eat*), f, w, u (as in *us* and *use*), v, n.

A **level-three** muffin tin might offer these letters: a (as in *at* and *ate*), p, pl, st, o (as in *otter* and *oat*), ch. When you get to level three, you may have to rephrase your question. If your child's penny lands on *st*, you should say, "Can you tell me what sounds those letters make?"

A **level-four** tin might hold these letters: oa, i (as in *it* and *ice*), nk, ft, z, spr.

A **level-five** tin might have these letters: au, oi, ee, sw, ar, d.

If you want to make other sets, turn to the appendix that lists "Important Sounds."

*B*efore your child plays SOUND CHECKERS, he must know how to play standard checkers. Many first-graders can be taught checkers. However, your child might not learn until the third grade. If that's the case, wait until then to play. SOUND CHECKERS helps children read even in the third grade.

When Joe heard he was going to work with the reading teacher, he was less than thrilled. He refused to accompany me to my workroom. I could have exerted my authority and demanded that he come with me, but that's a poor way to begin a working relationship. I played it cool. "Oh, come on, Joe. We won't do any work; we'll play a game of checkers."

That got him. Joe started coming to my workroom on a regular basis. After a week or two, I realized the flaw in this strategy. Regular checkers wasn't doing much for Joe's reading. I needed to tinker with the rules.

I began with a new checkerboard. I taped a small piece of paper with a letter written on it to each black square. The board then looked like this:

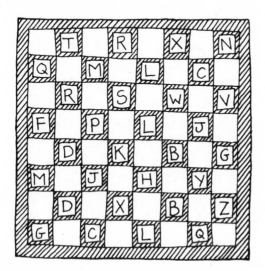

MATERIALS

checker board and pieces
pen
scissors
transparent tape
paper

As you can see, all the letters are facing in the same direction. I figured that I could read the letters upside down; Joe was having a hard enough time reading them right side up. When the board was ready, I went to Joe's classroom. "Are we going to play checkers today?" Joe asked, as soon as he saw me. "Sure," I said. "Only today it's a special game. Come along and I'll show you."

I presented Joe with the newly designed board and explained that checkers in its new form would help him to learn letter sounds. Joe hesitated, but after I explained the rules, he agreed to try. There is only one difference between SOUND CHECKERS and regular checkers. Before moving to a square, the player has to say the letter sound taped to that square. If the player can't say the sound, he still gets to make his move; in SOUND CHECKERS there are no punishments for mistakes—just words of praise for success.

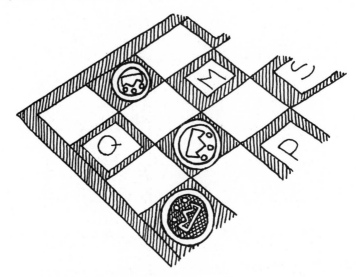

Above is a segment of a game in progress. It was Joe's move. He wanted his black checker to jump my red checker. Joe couldn't remember the sound for *m*. I told him the sound before he jumped me. Then, before jumping him back, I told him the sound *s* makes.

Identifying letter sounds makes SOUND CHECKERS a little slower than regular checkers. But SOUND CHECKERS is just as pleasant to play, and Joe was enthusiastic about it. For the first time, he was learning letters and sounds in a way that delighted him.

Joe started SOUND CHECKERS with easy sounds. But as we continued to play, I filled the board with harder and harder sounds. Here are sample boards at five levels of difficulty. If you want to make your own SOUND CHECKERS boards, use the "List of Important Sounds" at the back of this book.

Level One

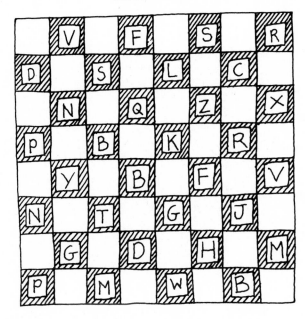

Level Two

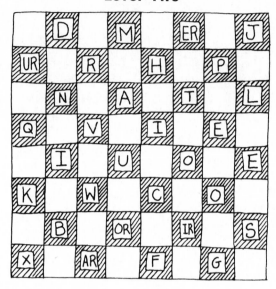

Level Three

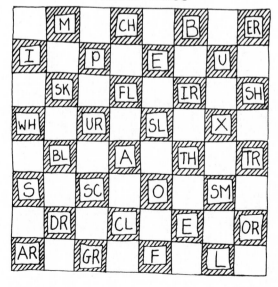

120

Level Four

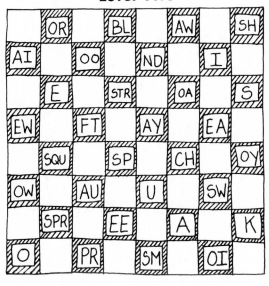

	J		E		U		GL
SH		DW		CL		TH	
	SHR		PL		OE		ND
AR		UE		ST		THR	
	I		AI		A		ER
NG		WH		SCR		FT	
	Y		O		G		SPL
C		SK		TW		CH	

Level Five

	OR		BL		AW		SH
AI		OO		ND		I	
	E		STR		OA		S
EW		FT		AY		EA	
	SQU		SP		CH		OY
OW		AU		U		SW	
	SPR		EE		A		K
O		PR		SM		OI	

chapter 7.

Making Words

The games in this chapter help children to sound out words. This is a difficult skill and children often need help mastering it. But don't play these particular games until the beginning of second grade—or even later. If your child has difficulty reading, wait until third grade.

The problem is this: every teacher has a different technique for teaching how to sound out words. The method offered in the following games may be a little different from what your child is getting in school, and to pile one method on top of another may make your child's task harder, not easier. So let school take care of the initial stages. When your child has advanced somewhat, that's the time to start playing these games. The games will give him practice and refine his skills. Your child will like the games better at a later date, too, which is important. There's no point in playing games your child doesn't enjoy. Onerousness is the enemy of learning.

WORDS IN A BAG gave Emily lots of practice sounding out words. We played this game many times over many weeks, and Emily never got bored. Your child might like this game as much as Emily did. If he does, you have a lot of WORDS IN A BAG to look forward to.

The game was easy to make. I cut ten index cards in half. On these twenty cards, I wrote ten segmented words.

MATERIALS

two bags
index cards
scissors
pen

After I wrote the words, I separated the word beginnings from the word endings. Then Emily and I went through both piles of cards, the beginnings pile and the endings pile, making sure she could read the sounds. I helped her with any sound that gave her trouble. Now we were ready to play. I put the beginnings in one bag, the endings in another, and gave both bags to Emily. She shook them up well, slipped her hand into the first bag, and

pulled out B . She put her hand into the second bag and came

up with UN . I asked her to read the cards separately. Then

I told her to fit the sounds together. BUN—Emily had picked a real word. She kept BUN on the table in front of her. Next I put my

hand into each bag. I pulled out N EN . I read the individual

cards aloud. Then I blended the sounds together. I wasn't as lucky as Emily. NEN isn't a word. I put NEN in front of me on the table. Emily took her second grab in the bag. She came out with

R   IM —another real word.

We continued picking until the bags were empty. When the final cards were on the table Emily had

B UN   R IM   C AT   T OD   N ED

While I had

N EN   H OP   P AP   S IT   T UP

Emily had picked four real words. (I let her use the proper name *Ned* as a word.) I had picked three real words. Actually I had to check *pap* in the dictionary because I wasn't sure if it was a real word. It is: *pap* is a soft food for babies. I didn't mind doing this extra work because it gave Emily living proof of how useful a dictionary can be. Our main concern, however, was the final tally—Emily 4, Peggy 3. Emily was the winner. In an effort to even the score, I suggested we play again. Emily was quick to agree. After all, she'd beaten me at my own game. Also, she'd found it easy to sound out bag words. With her confidence at a peak, we put the word segments back in the bags and started picking all over again. We could have used the same twenty cards time after time and still discovered new words. But there are good reasons to switch cards occasionally. Switching cards gave Emily a chance to work with new and different sounds. And once Emily was comfortable with three-letter words, I could throw some words with four letters into the bags. Here are six different WORDS IN A BAG games ready for you to copy.

Box 1

C	AB	G	EM	B	IG
J	OB	H	UM	S	AD
K	EG	H	IM	H	OT
	R	UB	

Box 2

R	AM	F	OG	D	IG
B	ED	J	UG	R	OB
H	ID	B	AG	P	UP
	S	ET	

Box 3

SK	IP	FL	AG	D	IM
CR	OP	SC	AT	J	UG
DR	OP	ST	OP	M	AD
	GL	AD	

Box 4

PL	UG	CL	AP	TR	IP
SL	ED	SP	OT	H	OP
CL	AM	ST	OP	B	UN
	K	IT	

Box 5

P	AN	R	OD	SL	IP
P	EG	B	UN	DR	OP
H	ID	B	AD	DR	UM
	R	ED	

Box 6

GR	IN	TR	IM	V	AN
CL	AP	SK	IT	W	AY
PR	OP	DR	IP	Y	ET
	SL	IM	

PICK
A BLEND

MATERIALS

blank paper
index cards
pen
scissors
optional: storage box

Bl, cl, fr, sm, st, dr, fl, gr, cr, spl, and scr are called "consonant blends." When you listen to st, you hear both the individual s and the individual t-sound. Nevertheless, the two letters blend together into one sound; that's why st is a consonant blend.

You may think that once a child knows the sound of s and the sound of t, blending the two sounds into st comes naturally. Some children do read consonant blends more or less automatically, but many stumble over these blends for months. PICK A BLEND makes learning blends a bit easier for such children. If your child doesn't stumble, play PICK A BLEND anyway. A little practice in blends never hurt anybody.

PICK A BLEND is played on two game boards. Each board has eight incomplete words written on it. The object is to complete the words by adding blends. A variety of blends are written on small cards that are spread out, face down, on the table. Players take turns picking one blend card at a time from anywhere on the table. If a player picks a blend that completes a word, he places the blend card on his playing board. If he picks a blend that doesn't complete a word, he returns the card face down to the table. The first player to fill in all eight words wins.

Here's how to make the game. Take six index cards and cut them into fourths. Write these blends on the cards.

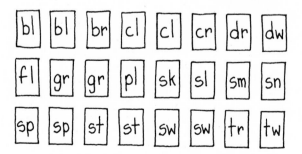

Take two sheets of blank paper and make these playing boards:

at	ack	ake	een
ar	ap	op	ope

een	esh	ip	im
un	am	ine	aim

Let your child pick one of the boards. Before starting the game, your child should read aloud the word endings on his board. If he has problems reading these sounds, that's OK. You can read for him when he needs the help.

Now you're ready to play. Spread the blend cards face down on the table. You go first, to show your child what to do. You pick the first blend. It might be *gr.* Start at the first square on your playing board. Hold the *gr* next to the *at* and read aloud, "*grat.*" *Grat* isn't a word. Move on to the next square. Place the *gr* next to the *ack* and read aloud, "*grack.*" Next try "*grake.*" Then, "*green.*" *Green* is a word. Leave the blend card right there. You have just filled in the first word on your playing board.

at	ack	ake	gr een
ar	ap	op	ope

Now it's your child's turn. He picks a blend and proceeds to try out words on his playing board. He reads each nonsense word aloud until he comes to a real word. From time to time his "real" word won't really be real. If he comes up with "crain," you'll have to tell him that the word that sounds like *crain* is spelled *crane*. On the other hand, he may read a real word like "*gram*" and not know it's real until you tell him. Sometimes a blend will go with more than one square—for instance, *flat, flack, flake, flap* and *flop*. Any of these will do. The next time you play, try switching game boards: the child takes yours and you take his. Here are three additional PICK A BLEND sets to pick and choose from. The last set is a bit more difficult, so save it for later.

Set One

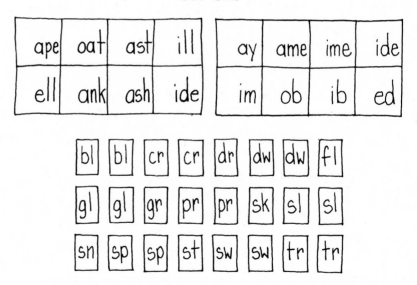

Set Two

ess	ing	ad	esh
ar	ab	all	at

all	ash	ig	ay
ess	ame	ar	ee

cl	cr	cr	dr	fl	fr	fr	gl

gl	pl	pr	pr	sc	sc	sc	sl

sm	sm	st	st	sw	sw	tr	tw

Set Three

eam	ub	imp	ill
ay	ing	are	eak

ed	int	ash	ead
ee	eet	int	out

dr	fr	gl	gr	pr	sc	scr	scr

shr	shr	sp	spl	spl	spr	spr	squ

squ	st	str	str	str	sw	thr	thr

CHAIN GAME

MATERIALS

pen and paper

*T*he idea here is to create the longest word chain possible. The chain begins with any random word. Short words are the easiest to work with—for instance, *mat.* The next word must differ from *mat* by one letter. *Met*, *mate*, or *malt* can all be used. *Mute*, *tam*, or *mitt* cannot—they differ from *mat* in too many ways. Your job is to think of each new word and write it down on a piece of paper. Your child's job is to read the word aloud. If he can't, the chain is broken. If you can't think of a new word to add to the chain (and you can't repeat words), the chain is, again, broken. Some chains break after two words. Some chains are still going strong after twenty, twenty-five, even thirty words. Once Emily and I made a chain that was fifty words long. What a great event that was!

As your child gets older, and reading chain words no longer represents a challenge, CHAIN GAME is still fun to play. Just alter the rules a little. Now you and your child take turns adding words to the chain. You write *ship*, he writes *hip.* You write *chip*, he writes *clip.* This version should keep both of you challenged for years.

Here are some sample chains of various lengths. I've cut most of them off arbitrarily. You can use these as starters and add to them if your child can read his way through. Or just use them as examples of how chains grow.

Mat-cat-sat-sap-sip-lip-lit-bit-bite-kite-kit-it-if-in-pin-pine-wine-wind-kind-mind-mend . . .

Jump-pump-plump-plum-slum-slam-slim-slime-lime-time-tame-name-same-lame-blame-flame-fame-fume-fuse-use-us-bus-bust-rust-just-jest-pest-past-paste . . .

Trunk-drunk-dunk-duck-deck-peck-pick-lick-lack-slack-slick-slice-lice-lace-ace-ice-dice-rice-race-rate-rare-care-scare-scar-scarf- (Can you think of another word? I can't.)

Can you rearrange these five letters and discover the mystery word?

MATERIALS

index cards
pen

I'm sure that, given time and thought, you can. But you must admit, it's a challenge.

Children who love the test of a hard thinking game love MYSTERY WORDS. Mark was such a child. Hard work aroused his interest. Of course, I started him with less mysterious words than the one above (it's *shoes*, if you haven't figured it out). We began with three-letter mysteries. I cut up index cards into letter-size bits. I held these bits so that Mark couldn't see and wrote

I mixed up the letters and placed them on the table for Mark to puzzle out.

Mark started shuffling the letters around. First he came up with

"Is that a word?" he asked.

"Well, read it and we'll see." Mark was able to sound out "ept."

"Sorry," I said. "Ept isn't a word." Mark looked grim but determined. He rearranged the letters and spelled

He sounded out "tep" and realized that this couldn't be the mystery word, either. Not wanting him to get discouraged, I gave a hint. "Tep isn't the mystery word. But the mystery word does have the e in the middle." Mark started moving letters again.

He read "pet." He'd done it. He'd discovered the mystery word.

It's best to begin, as I did with Mark, by using three-letter words like cat, map, cup, lid, bad, bed, bud, tip, top, and so on. Sometimes three letters will make more than one word; for example, cat and act. Occasionally three letters will make three words: pat—tap—apt. I took advantage of these situations and asked Mark to find the extra mystery words. When the mystery of three-letter words seems easy for your child, introduce him to words with four letters. Eventually you might give him some five-letter words. Your experience with EHSSO should tell you how hard five-letter mysteries are to solve.

BACKWARDS

I played this game with Mike. I wasn't sure he would like the game, so the first time we played BACKWARDS I kept my fingers crossed and hoped for the best.

"Mike, I have a word I want you to sound out. When you've read the word, I'll tell you something about it that will surprise you."

I wrote EKIM on a piece of paper. It wasn't easy for Mike to sound out this word. At first he came up with "*Uckem.*"

"Good try, but let me help you get it exactly right." I covered all the letters except EK. "Can you tell me what sound EK makes?" Mike told me. "Great, now look at these letters." I covered the EK and exposed the IM. "Can you read this?" Mike read, "*Em.*" "That's almost it. Actually it says *im.* Now can you put the two parts together?" Mike sputtered, "*Ekim.*" So far he wasn't enthusiastic about this game. But then I said, "*Ekim,* do you know that's your name spelled backwards?"

Suddenly Mike smiled. Seizing the moment, I asked, "Would you like to read your last name backwards?" Mike nodded yes. I breathed a sigh of relief and wrote NAMTRAH . After *Namtrah,* he read, backwards, his brother's name, my name, and his mother's name. That was enough for one day. On other days we reversed food names, names of animals, and even the name of a superhero or two—hooray for *Namrepus!*

I've found that the easiest way to write backwards is to start at the right and spell to the left, like writing Hebrew. After you are expert at the writing and your child is a pro at backwards reading, you might try writing entire sentences, for instance:

EMIT AZZIP SI TI KNIHT I

MATERIALS

paper
pen

PART THREE

Games for Understanding

chapter 8.

What Does That Mean?

Nina was feeling discouraged. Until the fourth grade, she'd kept up with her classmates in reading—but then she fell behind. She was sent to me for an evaluation, and I found, among other problems, that her vocabulary was weak. I wasn't surprised. When a child reads reasonably well in earlier years but falls behind in the fourth, fifth, or sixth grade, poor vocabulary is almost always a culprit.

How do vocabulary problems go unnoticed until the fourth grade? In early grades children learn to read hundreds of words, but for the most part, they know the meaning of these words already. Vocabulary-building is not part of the classroom curriculum, and books written for the early grades don't stress unusual or difficult words. This situation reverses in later grades; books for upper elementary students include many new vocabulary words. Children with good vocabularies take this in stride; but children with weak vocabularies stumble at the new demands.

You don't have to wait until your child reaches fourth grade to strengthen his vocabulary. You can start right now—for instance, by fostering an interest in language. Young children are fascinated by words. "What does that mean?" is practically a young child's chant. This curiosity about words helped your child master speech as an infant. But you have to nurture the curiosity or it will fade in later years.

There are three ways you can encourage this interest. One is to read aloud to your child. Reading aloud stimulates an interest in words and language. When you read to children, they get to hear language they might not be ready to read for themselves. Your child might be limited for the moment to reading relatively simple books; meanwhile, you can read aloud to him works by the best writers. Could there be better vocabulary teachers than A. A. Milne and *Winnie the Pooh*, or E. B. White and *Charlotte's Web*?

A second thing you can do is to avoid talking down to your child. Use the same grown-up vocabulary with children that you do with everyone else. When your child doesn't understand a word, you should feel delighted to explain it.

The third tactic is to play the games in this chapter, which are designed to whet your child's appetite for words. Most of the games are word contests. One game includes storytelling. Another involves playing with a children's dictionary, which is a lot of fun. You may find some of these games genuinely taxing. The best time to play may well be some other moment than when you stagger home from work, head reeling. Nevertheless, it's good to play games that are intellectually stimulating—for you as well as for your child. Let your youngster see your poor, exhausted, grown-up brain struggle a little; it'll do the child good.

SEE IT — NAME IT

You can play this game anytime you and your child find yourselves sitting around with nothing special to do.

"Refrigerator," Anita said.
"Linoleum," said I.
"Sink," said Anita.
"Colander," said I.
"Ice."
"Faucet."
"Stove."
"Detergent."
Anita asked, "What does *detergent* mean?"
"*Detergent*," I told her, "is a word that means strong soap—for instance, dishwashing detergent."

This game is called SEE IT—NAME IT. You may remember LABEL THE HOUSE in Chapter One. SEE IT—NAME IT is the same game played without labels. You and your child sit in a room and list everything you see. Your child will probably begin with easy-to-spot items like *refrigerator, sink*, and *stove*. You should contribute the less obvious items, such as *detergent, faucet*, or *colander*. Encourage your child to ask the meaning of unknown words. Don't limit yourself to names of whole objects; you can include parts of objects as well. Here are some words I came up with while looking at a stove: *oven, broiler, racks, pilot light, flame, gas, enamel, chrome, handle, burner, thermometer, hinges, runners*. Getting a child to look intensely at a stove helps him learn more words. Careful looking also develops visual awareness.

Don't feel that going through the kitchen once like this means that you can't do it again. In fact, a child will only learn words like *spatula, thyme*, and *strainer* by hearing them again and again.

You can play SEE IT—NAME IT three different ways. You and your child can work together on listing as many words as possible in five minutes. Speed and quantity are your goals. A second way is to work together to reach a set number of words. Try to think of thirty kitchen words, or forty living-room words, or fifty bedroom words. The third way is to make as long a list as you can with no time limits. The game ends when one player runs out of words.

One day Anita couldn't think of a new kitchen word. "I don't know what to add to the list."

I decided to help her out. "What's that yellow thing on the sink?"

"That's a sponge."

"Great, we're up to word number 65."

GO-TOGETHERS

Sometimes good ideas pop out of nowhere. That's the way it was with GO-TOGETHERS. I had been working with Alma for almost a year. She had a variety of reading problems, not the least of which was a limited vocabulary. As a result of the work we'd done and the games we'd played, Alma had made good progress. One day, however, I was all played out. I couldn't think of a single new teaching idea, and there was Alma staring at me, asking what we were going to do next. I glanced out the window and saw the fourth-graders playing baseball. Aha! A variation of SEE IT—NAME IT popped into mind.

"Let's list all the baseball words we can. Whoever runs out of words first, loses the game."

Alma warmed to this idea immediately. She said bat, I said pitcher, she said bases, I said stadium, she said outfield, I said World Series, and on it went. GO-TOGETHERS was a success. After this first game. GO-TOGETHERS became a regular feature of my vocabulary-teaching routine.

Any category that strikes your imagination can be the basis for a GO-TOGETHERS game:

> types of cars—*Buick, station wagon, jeep* . . .
> supermarket words—*shopper, cash register, fruit* . . .
> winter words—*sleds, snow, cold* . . .
> angry words—*horrible, furious, I hate you* (as "I hate you" shows, you can use phrases instead of single words) . . .

Include some unfamiliar words. In a supermarket list, you might add words such as *bargain, quality, concentrated, merchandise,* or *premium.* When your child asks the meaning of any word, tell him. But don't get carried away with unknown words; three new words per game is a maximum limit.

Sometimes the list ends abruptly after only two or three words. That's OK. As long as you and your child are enjoying the game, pick a new category and start again. Sometimes a category seems interminable. Once Alma and I listed terrible smells. The list grew longer and longer: cigarette smoke, mildew, burnt food, dirty laundry, garbage, sewage, vomit, liver cooking, bad breath, cat litter, rotten milk, burning rubber, onions . . . Finally we declared a tie. It's amazing how many terrible smells there are in the world.

STORY WORDS

OPTIONAL MATERIALS

paper and pencil

Your child starts this game by thinking of three words. Any three words will do:

baseball   tangerine   table

Using these words you make up a short story:

One day I was playing *baseball.* I hit a home run. When the game was over, I was hot and hungry. I went to my house. I got a *tangerine.* I ate the tangerine at the kitchen *table.* The tangerine tasted delicious.

Now switch parts. It is you who come up with three words and your child makes up the story:

baboon   skyscraper   sneakers

In the beginning, your child may have a hard time thinking up stories. If he needs help, suggest a starting sentence. "Once a *baboon* decided to visit New York City." If he has trouble keeping the story going, make more suggestions. "Maybe the *baboon* could wear *sneakers* during his visit to New York."

When your child learns to handle three words, add one more. When he can handle four words, try five. You can write the words on a piece of paper so you won't forget them.

song   pencil   chair   teacher   very

I went to my classroom and sat on a *chair.* My *teacher* was *very* busy. She was singing a *song.* We had to write out the song with a *pencil.*

Try including an unknown word or two among the starter words. Define the unknown word and use it in a sentence:

apple tree   famished   jogging

"*Famished* means very hungry. 'I hadn't eaten all day, so I was *famished* at dinnertime.' "

Keep alternating roles as word giver and storyteller. Continue playing until one of your is fed up with stories. Then it will be time for something else—for instance, bedtime.

A FRUMDIDDLE

A frumdiddle is a secret object (*sofa*), a plant (*violet*), or an animal (*zebra*). When you play the game, one person must think of a frumdiddle and offer clues to what it is, while the other person must guess. You give a clue, and your child guesses; if he doesn't guess right, you provide another clue, and your child guesses again. Naturally, you should use obvious clues for a child new to frumdiddling and graduate to obscure clues as the child gets better at the game.

One day, playing with Ian, my frumdiddle was a cat.

Peggy: My frumdiddle can fit inside a shopping bag.
Ian: Is it an ice cream cone?
Peggy: No, it can fit in a shopping bag and it has four legs.
Ian: Is it a horse?
Peggy: No, a horse has four legs but can't fit into a shopping bag. You can take another guess for this clue.
Ian: Is it a turtle?
Peggy: No, my frumdiddle can fit inside a shopping bag, it has four legs, and it is furry.
Ian: Is it a cat?
Peggy: *Frumdiddle!*

Frumdiddle clues are an occasion to stretch your child's vocabulary. Instead of saying your frumdiddle is *big*, say it is *huge, enormous, gigantic, grand, titanic, massive,* or *immense.* Instead of saying it's *small*, say it is *tiny, minuscule, petite, diminutive, puny, slight,* or *teeny-weeny.* Instead of saying it's *red*, say it is *crimson,* the color of a *pomegranate, scarlet,* or *maroon.* A few vocabulary stretchers add challenge to the game, but too many make the game boring. A couple or perhaps three unknown words per game is a good number.

And remember to say, when a child guesses right, "Frumdiddle!" This is the child's reward. He gets to hear you say something ridiculous.

MATCHES AND OPPOSITES

Agood way to increase a child's vocabulary is to teach words for one idea.

Here's how you do it. You say a word and your child tries to think of a matching word. Then he says a word, and you think of a match.

> small—little
> big—huge
> sad—depressed
> silly—funny
> strange—weird
> scary—spooky
> beautiful—gorgeous

"Sofa," I said.

Carolyn thought a moment. "Couch!" she said, and I nodded approval. Now it was her turn to propose a word. "Walk," she said.

I pondered. "Stroll!"

"What does stroll mean?" she asked.

I told her stroll means to walk in a leisurely way. Next it was my turn to suggest a word. "Street."

"Road," she replied.

This game is more challenging than you'd think. There are some words that can't easily be matched by either children or adults. Not even Webster can match certain words. That's why you should be flexible about what constitutes an acceptable answer.

> shoe—slipper
> draw—scribble
> chair—bench
> huge—tall

These may not be perfect synonyms, but they'll do.

Eventually, either you or your child will come upon a word that won't be matched, not even by an imperfect synonym. Offhand, I can't think of a match for *rainbow*. Maybe if I thought and thought I could, but the hard work of thinking and thinking would take away from my pleasure in the game. What's more, a long delay might lose the child's attention. That's why a time limit is a good idea. If a matching word doesn't come to mind by the count of, say, twenty, then the word is declared unmatchable. When a word is unmatchable, the game doesn't end; it is transformed. The player who can't think of a match proposes a brand-new word. But now his partner doesn't try to come up with a matching word. The hunt this time is for an opposite word.

"Rainbow," I said. And since Carolyn couldn't think of a synonym, she had to propose a new word.

"Up," she said.

I had to think of an opposite. "Down," I said. Now it was my turn to offer a word. We were still on opposites. "White," I said.

"Black," said Carolyn. I nodded approval. She proposed "in."

"Out," said I, and suggested "coffee."

"Tea," said Carolyn.

I thought about this. I guess *tea* really is a kind of opposite of *coffee*, so I agreed.

When a player can't think of an opposite word, that player must propose a new word. Then you go back to finding words that match.

Matching words, opposite words—the game goes on forever, or at least until the TV commercial is over, or hair is finally washed.

DICTIONARY READING

MATERIALS

a children's dictionary—
the type called "children's,"
not a "beginner's" or "first"
dictionary

*T*here are two types of dictionaries for elementary-school children. The "first" or "beginner's" dictionary is appropriate from kindergarten through second grade. A "children's" dictionary is geared for third- through sixth-graders. A beginning reader should probably own both types, if you can afford it. The beginner's dictionary is for his own use. The more advanced dictionary is for you and your child to make use of together. For instance, you might read aloud from this more-advanced dictionary. Read a dictionary? Yes indeed. Reading—or, rather, skimming—a dictionary is a terrific way to generate an interest in words.

Pick a quiet moment in the day, sit with your child on the sofa, and start leafing through the book. Look for new and interesting words. I think you'll be surprised by the variety you'll find. There's *gnu*, an animal similar to an antelope, which lives in Africa; there's *blunderbuss*, an old-time hunting gun with a funny-looking muzzle; there's *minaret*, a tall, slender tower on top of a mosque . . .

Initially you'll be the prime mover in this activity. You'll skim the pages and pick out intriguing words, you'll read and explain the words and definitions, and your interest and enthusiasm will carry the child along.

"See that word? That says *sphinx*, and here is a picture of a sphinx. Thousands of years ago, the Egyptians built huge sphinx statues. A sphinx has the body of a lion and the head of a man. Do you think there could ever be a real sphinx? Maybe we could get one for a pet. It would be like having a giant talking cat."

Eventually your child will take the lead at discovering words and reading definitions aloud. But there's no need to rush. Whoever reads, this activity shows your child that words are wonderful. And it stimulates a very useful affection for dictionaries. "*Dictionary*: a book that has words of a language arranged in alphabetical order, together with information about them. . . ."

chapter 9.

Making Sense

Children must come to understand the meaning not only of words, but also of sentences, paragraphs, and entire stories. They must understand the simple facts—for instance, *Rover swallowed a turtle.* They must understand the thrust of the narrative—understand it well enough to predict what might happen next. *I think Rover will go see a vet.* They'll be expected to reason sensibly about why something might have happened. *The vet took an x-ray so he could see the turtle in Rover's stomach.* They'll need to develop insights into the personalities of story characters. *The turtle is stubborn because he won't leave Rover's stomach.* They'll have to grasp the story's main idea. *Dogs should be careful not to confuse turtles with dog biscuits.*

These skills are the basis of reading comprehension. You can't read without comprehension; you can only recite. Unfortunately, many children merely recite. They decipher the letters and say the words, but don't understand what they're reading. These children need to be instructed, encouraged—and played with properly. Even children with good reading comprehension skills can benefit from a little help.

Of the following games, the first couple help children to understand the structure of sentences. The next pair of games get children thinking about story plots. All in all, the games will help children to achieve a better understanding of Rover, the vet, the turtle—the whole kit and kaboodle. That's the goal of reading comprehension.

TAKING TURNS

One day Elizabeth read aloud, "Betty wanted a dog. Her friend David had a dog named Tiger. Her friend Mary had a little puddle named Roger. Betty wanted a dog, too."

Elizabeth's reading *puddle* for *puppy* didn't concern me; anyone can make a mistake. I was concerned, however, that she didn't notice her mistake. Unfortunately, "puddles" named Roger, and similar errors, were a regular feature of Elizabeth's reading. For some reason, these nonsensical sentences didn't bother her. She didn't recognize the problem and therefore couldn't correct it.

TAKING TURNS addresses problems like Elizabeth's. I explained to her that TAKING TURNS is a way to share talking. I started a sentence; she finished it. Our first attempts at TAKING TURNS went like this:

Peggy: The elephant left the zoo because—
Elizabeth: there weren't any more peanuts.
Peggy: When I play checkers—
Elizabeth: I always win.
Peggy: I love winter when—
Elizabeth: there is snow and I can go sledding.

Sometimes Elizabeth took the first half of the sentence:

Elizabeth: I like the park because—
Peggy: there are so many trees.
Elizabeth: I wish I could—
Peggy: fly like a bird.

Here is a second, more difficult version of TAKING TURNS. I gave the end of a sentence and Elizabeth gave the beginning. To indicate the omitted portion, I clapped my hands.

Peggy: *clap*—so I went home.
Elizabeth: I was hungry, so I went home.
Peggy: *clap*—is my favorite food.
Elizabeth: Spaghetti is my favorite food.

Peggy: *clap*—because I see animals.
Elizabeth: I like to go to the zoo because I see animals.

A third way to play is to leave out the middle of the sentence:

Peggy: Today I am—*clap*—because it is hot.
Elizabeth: Today I am going swimming because it is hot.
Peggy: I am going to—*clap*—for Halloween.
Elizabeth: I am going to go trick-or-treating for Halloween.
Peggy: Elephants like—*clap*—for dinner.
Elizabeth: Elephants like peanuts for dinner.

The sentences can be funny:

> The polar bear was angry because—a fly punched him in the stomach.
> The lion turned green—because he ate a hundred pounds of string beans.

But it's a rule of TAKING TURNS that even ridiculous thoughts must make a certain kind of sense. They must sound plausible. "I like hot dogs because—swimmers dive into water" is not acceptable. TAKING TURNS sentences also have to follow grammatical rules. "The lions are—in his cage" won't do.

When Elizabeth made a mistake, I helped her to correct herself:

"I like hot dogs because— Can you give a reason why I like hot dogs?"

"Which sounds better: The lions are in *his cage* or the lions are in *their cages*?"

Usually this little bit of help got Elizabeth back on the track. And if she couldn't think of a way to complete a sentence, I threw out hints:

"The lions are— What might the lions be doing? Where are the lions right now? What do the lions look like? The lions are—"

All this shared playing helped Elizabeth recognize her reading mistakes.

"A puddle named Roger? Uh oh, something's wrong. . . ."

MISTAKES

Mistakes, mistakes, these are all mistakes.

> I write with an eraser.
> I like salty ice cream.
> My cat is hard and furry.

The question is, can your child discover the mistakes? Think of a confused sentence like one of those above, say it out loud, and let your child correct you. Children love to correct adults: this game has built-in appeal.

> A carpenter works in a laundry.
> A watch tells color.
> I turn lights off when it gets dark.
> A mouse is enormous.

After your child gets good at correcting sentences, try telling some stories that have mistakes:

"When Burt got dressed in the morning, he put on his shirt and then his pants, his shoes and then his socks. He combed his hair and went into the kitchen for breakfast."

Or:

"Once a man bought lots of groceries at the supermarket. He bought ice cream, cookies, chicken, bread, jelly, peanut butter, and carrots, but when he got home he was angry because he had forgotten to buy dessert."

Here are some more mistake stories you can try out on your child:

> Jason went to the beach. He went swimming, lay in the sun, hunted for sea shells, and built a snowman.

> On Halloween, Joyce went trick-or-treating. She dressed as a witch. She had a broom, a big black hat, a

sparkly halo, a black gown, and a pair of black pointy shoes.

Yvonne was drawing a picture. She wanted to draw a garden in spring, but she didn't have a yellow crayon to draw the sun. She decided to draw yellow daffodils instead.

Jill was talking about her favorite colors with Eric. Eric said his favorite color was brown. Jill said her favorite color was blue. Jill said she likes to eat blueberries because they are blue. Eric said he likes strawberries because they are his favorite color.

My cat sits on my lap every day. He likes it when I scratch his stomach. He purrs and purrs. Her favorite food is tuna fish. I have to hide my tuna-fish sandwiches from her so that she doesn't try to eat them up.

One day I told Paul a mistake story. He hated it. For him, there wasn't any pleasure in trying to figure out the mistake. He felt that I was testing him, not playing with him. So that was Paul's one and only mistake story. If a game's no fun, why play? On the other hand, Zara loved finding the mistakes in mistake stories. The more stories I could make up, the happier she was. To each his own.

FINISH A
FAIRY TALE

MATERIALS

a book of fairy tales
(the appendix of
"Books for Reading Aloud"
includes some good
fairy tale collections)

You are reading an Agatha Christie mystery, when suddenly you have to get up and do something else. What happens to the mystery? You try to finish it in your own mind. Your formidable adult powers of analysis are brought to bear on the supreme question, whodunit? Children must be taught to make this kind of analysis, to think closely about what they read, to remember details, to make predictions on the basis of what has already been said. These are basic elements of reading comprehension. Interrupting a story and trying to guess what happens next is a good way to develop such skills. But with children, don't use mysteries; use fairy tales. Start to read aloud and suddenly . . . STOP. Your child must guess what happens next. Does Jack climb the beanstalk? Your child might not come up with the correct answer. He might think that Jack cuts the beanstalk and burns it. That's OK; in fact, that's great. As long as the answer is consistent with the story up until that moment, your child is doing fine.

Fairy tales are good for guessing about because they have a predictable form combined with elements of fantasy and magic. Fairy tales also move along at a rapid clip. You don't have to read very far in a fairy tale to get an idea where the plot is going. That's the time to stop reading and ask, "Well, what do you think will happen next?"

One day, working with a small reading group, I kept interrupting a story about Simpleton and his brothers:

"Two king's sons went out in search of adventure and fell into a wild, disorderly way of living, so that they never came home again. The king's youngest son, who was called Simpleton, set out to seek his brothers. But when he finally found them, they laughed at him for thinking that a simple fellow like himself could get through the world, when clever fellows like themselves had so much trouble. They all three traveled away together, and came to an anthill. The two older brother wanted to destroy the anthill, to see the little ants creeping about in terror. . . ."

I stopped to ask, "What do you think happens next?"

Elizabeth answered, "I think the King of the Ants turns the brothers into dust."

"Good guess. It's not what happens, but it is a good idea. What happens is . . .

"Simpleton said, 'Leave the creatures in peace; I won't allow you to disturb them.' Then they went onward and came to a lake where a great number of ducks were swimming. The two brothers wanted to catch a couple and roast them. . . .'"

I stopped again and asked, "Now what happens?"

This time Alberto answered. "I think the ducks like to swim."

Alberto needed a little help in focusing his guess. I said, "Yes, I think the ducks like to swim. But right now the brothers are thinking about catching the ducks and cooking them. What do you think will happen? Will they kill the ducks?"

Alberto tried again: "I think the ducks will fly away."

"That's a good guess, an excellent guess. It isn't what happens, though. Here is what really happens. . . ."

And so it went until the end of the story, at which point everyone knew what would happen next:

"And they all lived happily ever after."

TV TALK

MATERIALS

a television set

*I*could rant and rave for page after page about the terrible effects of television on children, but the truth is this: TV is here to stay. So here's one way to make the best of it.

One day I overhead Sean talking about a TV show. He was so alert and animated that I stopped to listen. His friend had missed the episode, and Sean was recounting the plot. The retelling was ordered and logical. Sean remembered the general outline of the story as well as significant details. I asked him a few questions about the show—questions of the kind that I usually ask children in reading class.

"Why do you think Lucy acted like that? If you were Desi, what would you have done? Why didn't Lucy tell Desi about buying new furniture? How did you know Lucy was fibbing?"

Then we began to discuss why Sean liked this show. We talked about what made it funny and exciting. It became clear that Sean rarely talked about the many hours of TV that he watched. But talking about the programs is one way to make TV-viewing useful. By talking about these shows, Sean learned to interpret and analyze stories with even more logic and insight than before. This could be called TV comprehension. The necessary skills of analysis, logic, and attention to detail are really no different from the skills required in reading comprehension.

Sean loved to talk about TV, but if he felt I was quizzing him, he clammed up. You can avoid this problem at home by watching shows together. As the story progresses, start to discuss the plot and characters. During commercials, see if your child can guess how Lucy will get out of this fix. Will Desi discover the secret? Will Ethel and Fred make up? Will Ethel help Lucy hide the furniture?

Questions that ask *who, what, where, when, why,* and *how* are good discussion-starters.

"*Why* did Archie scream at Edith like that?"

"He was angry with her."

"Maybe, but she really hadn't done anything."

"Well, Archie yells anyway."

"But *what* makes him yell?"

"Maybe he can't think of how else to talk."

"Sometimes I yell because I want to get my own way; other times I yell if I'm frustrated."

"I think Archie yells because he likes to get his own way."

"*How* does Edith get her way?"

"I don't know. She just does things. Maybe she doesn't get her way."

"If you were Edith, what would you yell?"

"I'd yell—ARCHIE, YOU DINGBAT!"

By now the commercial is probably over and Archie is up to his old shenanigans.

chapter 10.

Imagination

The games in this chapter are different from those in other chapters. These games don't teach specific things like the sound for *b*. Instead, they nurture something just as important in learning to read but less tangible—a child's imagination and ability to express this imagination in words.

We don't normally think of imagination as a part of reading. But it's not enough to have technical skill with words and sentences and to be able to make sense of narrative. To read properly, you have to take the words from the page and vividly picture what they mean in your mind's eye. You have to translate, that is, from written words to imagined vistas.

Some children already have a splendidly active imagination and find it easy to express their imaginative thinking in words. They are the spirited talkers and storytellers. But there are a great many children, sometimes very bright ones, who could use a push to develop their powers of imagination. And there are children whose imagination is keen, but who rarely put their fantastic thoughts into words. These children benefit a good deal from the right kind of play. The games in this chapter require children to make up stories, to picture characters, to describe faraway places, to concoct preposterous events—all activities to stretch the imagination into words.

These games call for a good bit of imagination on the parent's part, too—perhaps more imagination than a person can summon up after a hard day's work. Is this the case with you? Then save these games for more imaginative days. The games should be as much fun for you as for your child; if they're not, don't play them.

CIRCLE STORY

You and your child are sitting in a restaurant; you've given the order and are waiting for the food. But your child is cranky and restless. What to do? You could start a CIRCLE STORY. Begin with a title that indicates what the story will be about. If your child has trouble thinking of a title, suggest two or three and let him pick his favorite. Any title will do—My Trip to Mars, The Invisible Superhero, If I Were a Magician. Once your child picks a title, you begin the story, but only for a sentence or two. Your child takes up where you leave off. He adds one or two more sentences and then stops so that you can have another turn. Keep taking turns until the story is finished. All this back-and-forth storytelling teaches children how stories develop and how one story idea connects with another. The game is an object lesson in the principles of narrative. And obviously, playing the game helps to stretch a child's imagination.

Here is a CIRCLE STORY Denise and I made up, called "Carol and the Tiger:"

Peggy: Once a girl named Carol went on a class trip to the zoo. Carol was excited about going to the zoo because . . .

Denise: She liked to see the tigers.

Peggy: When Carol got to the tiger cage, she was so busy looking at the tigers that she didn't notice that her class had walked away. She was alone with the tigers when suddenly . . .

Denise: When suddenly one tiger turned and said, "Hello."

Peggy: Carol was amazed, but she remembered her manners and said hello to the tiger.

Denise: The tiger smiled.

Peggy: The tiger asked if Carol wanted to ride on his back.

Denise: Carol said yes.

Peggy: Carol opened the cage door, walked over to the tiger, and climbed on his back. She and the tiger left the cage and started walking around the zoo. Then they went into the street, where they saw a robber.

Denise: Carol said, "Let's chase that robber."

Peggy: They caught the robber. All the people cheered.
Denise: Carol and the tiger got medals.
Peggy: Carol's classmates saw the tiger get the medal.
Denise: They saw Carol get a medal, too.
Peggy: Carol went home to tell her mother and father.
Denise: The end.

The story went smoothly. Denise and I were old hands at this game. Beginners, however, and even experienced CIRCLE STORY tellers, may run into problems. Children often find it hard to think of a new story idea. It's easy to get stuck with nothing to say. If your child has this problem, try stopping your own contribution at the edge of a cliff: "She was alone with the tigers when suddenly . . ." Now your child has simply to finish your thought rather than face the more difficult task of coming up with an idea on his own. Another pitfall occurs when a child makes an inappriate contribution:

Peggy: Carol said hello to the tiger.
Denise: Carol's mother likes ice cream.

If this happens, ask your child to think about the whole story.

Peggy: Carol is at the zoo looking at the tigers when this surprising thing happens: the tiger says hello to Carol. Carol says hello to the tiger. What do you think the tiger will say to Carol next?

HELLO!

Whenever possible, let your child take the initiative in plotting the story. Encourage the child's ideas and imagination by following through on his story line. If he lands a spaceship on Mars, stay on Mars; if he takes off for Venus, head on to Venus. Your contributions can add excitement and variety if the story begins to get dull.

Should food come to the table before the story ends, you will want to speed things along. Tell your child it's time to think of a good ending, and then make your own contribution a quick lowering of the curtain:

> And so the boy ran home.
> The girl hit the monster and the monster fell down dead.
> Gregory lost his magic powers and went home for dinner.

CIRCLE STORY can be played with lots of people. In fact, you can make up a CIRCLE STORY with a whole birthday party of children waiting for the cake. Children like to pass a story from child to child. I remember one from my class: about Carlos, who had a magic ice cream cone.—Carlos could make any wishes he wanted before the ice cream melted.—Just as the ice cream was about to melt,—a wicked wizard came.—He stole the ice cream and trapped Carlos in the dungeon . . .

Your turn.

CRAZY ANSWERS

*T*his game encourages verbal flights of fancy. A good time to play is when you might otherwise be utterly bored: for instance, while cleaning the house, setting the table, or waiting for the bus to arrive.

Why do tigers have stripes?
How do birds fly?
How does a TV work?
What is electricity?
What is a spider's web?
Where do pineapples come from?

I'm sure you've faced your share of such questions. Usually it's good to answer seriously and give your child useful information. But now and then, try forgetting about being useful. Tell your child that for now you are going to respond to serious questions with answers that are make-believe, loony, and weird. Tell him that after you make up a crazy answer, he can make one up, too.

Begin with a question about how the world works—for example, "how do trees get leaves?" Then start inventing crazy answers. "Trees get leaves from a good witch. Every spring she cuts out billions of leaves from leaf cloth. Then she dyes the leaves green. She gives them to thousands of elves. These elves have magic glue. They go around the world gluing leaves to the trees." Or, "Trees get leaves because squirrels have little leaf seeds on their feet. They leave these seeds all over the trees. The seeds sprout when the weather gets warm." Another crazy answer might start with the question, "why do cats purr?" "I'm sure cats purr because there is a motor inside. Of course, they may purr because they swallow broken whistles. Or perhaps the purr is what's left of the birds they've eaten."

Your child will use your crazy answers as a model for inventing his or her own. That's why the more imaginative and far-out your answers are, the kookier your child's answers will be. And the kookier the better—because in this game, kookiness stretches the imagination.

You must be prepared, of course, with a lot of questions. At the beginning of this activity, I listed several. Here are some others: Why is the sky blue? Why do stars shine? Where does the moon go during the day? How deep is the ocean? How are crayons made?

"Denise, why is the grass green? Give me a crazy answer."

"A crazy answer? OK, let's see. The grass is green because one day . . ."

TALL TALES OF YOUR DAY

MATERIALS

And to Think That I Saw It on Mulberry Street
(a picture book by Dr. Seuss)

Sonia had a superactive imagination. She spent most of her time daydreaming. Unfortunately, she kept her imaginary world to herself. On rare occasions, teachers and other adults got a glimmer of her fantasy life, but she had few friends and didn't often play with other children. As a result, Sonia possessed an overdeveloped imagination, but an underdeveloped ability to use language. This language difficulty made it hard for her to learn to read.

Sonia needed to talk. One way to get her talking was to encourage her to share her imaginary world. I recruited the one and only Dr. Seuss to help do this. Dr. Seuss is the author of, among other children's classics, *And to Think That I Saw It on Mulberry Street.* This book tells the story of Marco, a boy with an imagination as active as Sonia's. Every day as Marco leaves for school, his Dad tells him to keep his eyelids up and see what he can see. And every day after school, Dad asks Marco what he has seen. Marco always tells Dad wild tales of incredible sights. The book shows Marco trying to decide what to tell his father on a day when, during his walk home, all he saw was a horse and wagon on Mulberry Street.

> "That *can't* be my story. That's only a *start.*
> I'll say a ZEBRA was pulling that cart!
> And that is a story that no one can beat,
> When I say that I saw it on Mulberry Street."

A zebra alone won't do, however. The zebra must pull a chariot with a charioteer. But a zebra is too small, so Marco decides that a reindeer is a better choice. The story gets more and more fantastic. Finally Marco fantasizes a pair of giraffes, an elephant, a royal Rajah, and a brass band—all part of a huge parade viewed by the entire city, including the mayor. Marco, in a fever of excitement, runs home. "FOR I HAD A STORY THAT *NO ONE* COULD BEAT!/ AND TO THINK THAT I SAW IT ON MULBERRY STREET!"

I read this book to Sonia. She was thrilled. A little boy inventing an enormous fantasy was something she could appreciate. I looked at Sonia and said, "You know what I did after school yesterday?" She gave me a suspicious look and asked what I'd done. I began a Marcoesque tall tale of my day.

"Right after school I got a phone call from my old friend Blanche. She invited me out for the afternoon. A visit with Blanche is always an adventure, so I said yes. Blanche told me to meet her at the airport. When I reached the airport, I saw Blanche's private jet waiting. Blanche directed the captain to take us to Hawaii. 'I know how much you like to swim,' she said. We landed in Hawaii and went to Blanche's private beach. On Blanche's beach the sand is all the colors of the rainbow. The water is crystal clear, so you can see every fish in the ocean. After we had a swim, Blanche said, 'I bet you're hungry.' We boarded the jet and flew to China. There we ate a twelve-course Chinese banquet. Then it was time for dessert. Off we jetted to Paris, France. While we were eating French pastry, a French movie director came up to me. He said he'd make me a movie star. I said thanks anyway, I'll stick to teaching. Then we flew home. It was very late at night when we arrived, so that's why I'm a little sleepy today."

Sonia's laughter showed how much she enjoyed my tall tale.

"Sonia, what did you do after school yesterday?" This was her chance. At first she was a little reluctant to say anything. I had to coax her. At a few points in her story, I had to ask, "And then what?" Nevertheless, out came an unmistakably tall tale. She went on a jet plane. She met the Queen of England. She was going to marry the Prince, but she remembered she had to feed her dog. Sonia's first tall tale was terrific; but even if it had been terrible, it would have been terrific. She made use of some ideas in my story, which was fine. To inspire her was the reason I'd told her my tall tale.

Sonia and I kept exchanging tall tales. With this encouragement, it wasn't long before private Sonia began to open up. As her use of language improved, so did her reading. Sonia discovered that books told wonderful stories. Soon she had two favorite activities—reading books and making up stories with friends.

I suggest that you begin tall tales with your child as I did with Sonia, by reading Dr. Seuss. Then launch into your own stories. First think of adventures you'd like to have—a trip to Africa, a flight to outer space, discovering a magic wishing stone. Begin with a basic idea: *Once I took a huge ocean liner to Africa.* Let the story flow: *In Africa, I found myself surrounded by a hundred elephants.* Take advantage of ideas from children's books: *The elephant leader had a golden crown on his head.* When your first fantasy is played out, tack on a second: *Suddenly a witch came and gave me a magic wand. . . .*

The only rule is to leave logic behind, and let whimsy take over.

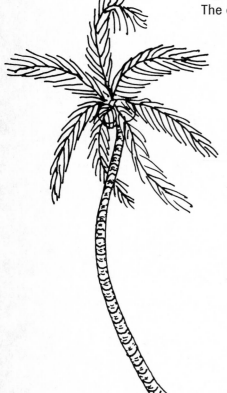

*T*his is an away-from-home game. Play it on a bus, in a restaurant, in the playground, or waiting in line for the movies.

Have you ever sat on a bus making up stories about the person sitting across from you? Perhaps that person is a baseball scout, looking for the next major league star; or a piano player on his way to give a concert; or a visitor from another planet—the possibilities are staggering. Letting your child pretend with you is another way to get him to articulate his thoughts and fantasies.

It takes a little practice to work up fantasies about strangers. Don't expect secret agents the first time you play. Start by picking out an interesting stranger. Ask your child not to stare or point—tell him the game must be a secret—and then ask questions about this stranger's life:

"You see that girl with the braids, sitting on the swing? I wonder what she likes to do when she's with her friends?"

Your child may protest, "I never met this girl in my life, so how should I know what she does with her friends?"

You can answer, "Well, this is just a pretend game. We're making up a life for her. I never met this girl either, but I'll guess she likes to play card games and card tricks. I think she knows lots of card tricks and likes to try them out on her friends. Can you guess something she really hates to do?"

"I think she hates to clean up her room."

"That's a good guess. Let's see, I think she hates to wash her hair. Her hair is so long I bet it balls up in knots and hurts when her mother combs it out. What do you think she likes best about school?" Keep the questions coming: Do you think she has a brother or a sister? Do they ever fight? Does she like to draw? What is the scariest thing she's ever done? What does she want to be when she grows up?

When your child has more experience in imagining a stranger's life, you can start telling little stories and skip the questions and answers. First you tell a story, then your child tells a story. You go first in order to prod the child's imagination.

"Do you see that man in the flower shop? I think he's buying flowers for his wife. They had a fight this morning. She was angry because he drank all the orange juice. He was angry because she didn't say she wanted juice, so why shouldn't he finish it? All day he felt bad about the fight, so now he's buying her tulips and half a gallon of juice in order to make up. Why do you think he is in the flower shop?"

Your child considers carefully and responds. "I know! He's buying flowers for his mommy."

*T*his is another game for in-between minutes in the day—after dinner and before homework, waiting for laundry to come out of the drier, while peeling potatoes.

"You are in a shipwreck. You manage to get to a deserted island. You're all alone. There are no people or animals on the island. There are large fruit trees, so you have food. You have no radio, no supplies of any kind. You know another ship will come near the island in roughly a month, but the ship may pass by without seeing you or stopping. What do you do?"

I confronted Nancy with this problem and asked her to come up with a solution. She replied, "I don't know what I'd do. That never happened to me." Here in a nutshell was Nancy's difficulty. She was too inhibited to throw herself into an imaginary situation. She couldn't picture herself in another world, couldn't pretend. If things stayed this way, how would she ever enjoy *Swiss Family Robinson* or *Treasure Island*? So I didn't accept her answer.

"Nancy, think about being all alone on a beach. There are no houses, no people. The only way you will ever get off the beach is to make sure a passing ship sees you. You have to think of something."

With this extra push, Nancy took a stab at the problem. "I'll make a big fire."

I liked this answer. But then I thought about it and decided I could get her to imagine a bit more. "That's a good idea, but how will you make a big fire? You don't have any matches. There are lots of trees for firewood, but you don't have anything with which to cut down the trees."

Nancy looked grave. "I'll rub sticks together, like a Girl Scout or an Indian, and start a fire that way. I'll pick up sticks on the ground to make the fire burn."

"Yes, but you need a really huge fire for the ship to see it. You don't know exactly when the ship is coming, so the fire may have to burn for a long time."

PROBLEMS AND SOLUTIONS

OPTIONAL MATERIALS

index cards
file box
pen

"I'll climb the trees. I'll get to the high branches that are easy to break, rip them off, and drop them to the ground. Then I'll have enough to burn. I'll stay at the top of the tree until I see the ship; then I'll start the fire. I'll eat the fruit in the trees until the ship comes."

Here was a thoughtful, imaginative solution to the shipwreck problem—a real breakthrough for Nancy. Although I helped Nancy think about the problem, I limited myself to developing her ideas rather than imposing ideas of my own. Remember that there are no right or wrong answers in this game, only one possible solution and then another possible solution. Don't be bossy. Take pleasure in your child's imagination and ideas.

Nancy got to the point where she loved thinking up solutions to these hypothetical problems. She was always ready to try one more. Of course, not all children enjoy such games. But many do. That's why I started a PROBLEMS AND SOLUTIONS file box. Every now and again I sat down with some index cards and wrote out a few problems. Then I stored the cards in a file box. With the file box on hand, I always had a problem ready to spring on Nancy or any other eager problem solver.

Here are some problems from my file box. You can use them to get your own problem box started.

You are on a space voyage. Your rocket ship is having mechanical problems. You need to find a place to repair the ship. You land on the planet Xexon, deep in the woods. You know there are people on the planet, but you don't know if they are peaceful or violent. Suddenly you hear voices. They are speaking a strange language. What do you do?

You are a scientist, experimenting with a secret formula. You drink some of the formula by mistake, and start to shrink. When you stop shrinking, you are only five inches tall. What do you do?

You are sleeping over at a friend's house. You never slept there before. You wake up in the middle of the night and can't fall back to sleep. What do you do?

You just got a new box of crayons. You are drawing, when suddenly everything you're drawn comes alive. The cat you drew turns into a real cat; the flower you drew turns into a real flower. The cat and the flower stay alive for half an hour—then they become drawings again. You decide to keep the crayons' magic a secret. One day you walk into your bedroom. There's your little brother, drawing with the magic crayons. He is almost finished drawing a ferocious-looking bear. What do you do?

You have just won a million dollars. What do you do?

You recently moved to a new neighborhood. You are walking your dog. Suddenly he escapes from his leash in order to chase a cat. You call his name and run after him, but he gets away. You can't find him. What do you do?

If you play enough games like this, eventually your child will find it perfectly natural to address difficult problems, construct more or less logical solutions, and express himself in imaginative ways—basic skills of the sort that go under the label "intelligence."

INTERVIEW WITH AN ALLIGATOR

OPTIONAL MATERIALS

spiral notebook
blank paper
pencil, crayons, or
colored markers
glue
pen

On a rainy day when your child moans about being bored, this game should be a pleasant relief for both of you.

"Where do you live, Mr. Pencil?"

"I live in a drawer with lots of other pencils."

"Is it a good place to live?"

"Sometimes it's good, but it is very crowded and the other pencils push and roll on top of you. Also, sometimes the other pencils stick you with their points by mistake, which hurts."

"What's the best part of being a pencil?"

"I like it when my owner takes me out of the drawer and writes with me. It tickles. But I don't like it when he has to erase something; that gives me a headache."

You have just been eavesdropping on a game I played with Paul. This was a game where Paul chose to be a specific person, animal, or object, and I asked him questions about his life. He answered the questions, all the while pretending to be a pencil or a rhinoceros or his baby-sitter or a rainbow.

I started this interview game with Paul because I couldn't understand why he was so resistant to reading. He knew how to read, but didn't get involved in stories or books. He hadn't yet developed the ability to jump into a story, to feel what the characters felt, to be engrossed in their lives. INTERVIEW WITH AN ALLIGATOR gave Paul a chance to let go of his own identity and jump into another identity—a pencil's, for instance.

It took Paul quite a while to learn to do this. Our first efforts were pretty lame.

"Mr. Rattlesnake, what do you like to eat?"

"I don't know what rattlesnakes like to eat."

I reminded Paul that in this game he was the rattlesnake and therefore anything he decided would be right. With practice, he got the idea. Still, his answers tended to be brief and unimaginative.

"Mr. Rattlesnake, do you have any friends?"

"Yes."

"Who are your friends?"

"I dunno."

"Do you visit any other rattlesnakes?"

"Yes."

I had to think up leading questions, questions that drew out Paul's ideas. Then I let him know how much I enjoyed his answers.

"What is a game you play with your rattlesnake friends?"

"We scare people."

"Oh my, how do you scare them?"

"We shake rattles at them."

"That would scare me all right."

"Yeah, then we hiss and spit, and people run away."

I tried to ask questions that would stretch his imagination.

"Mr. Rattlesnake, do you have any magic powers?"

"Yes."

"What powers do you have?"

"I can become invisible."

"Do you ever trick other animals when you become invisible?"

"One day I tricked a big elephant. First I was invisible. I went right under his trunk and jumped up and became visible. He was so scared, he ran away."

Sometimes I gave Paul a chance to interview me. Once I decided to be Miss Piggy. Paul had lots of interview questions to ask. "Do you really like Kermit? Can you really speak French? Why don't you go on a diet? Do you like being on TV?"

The success of INTERVIEW WITH AN ALLIGATOR depends on a child's choice of character. Any person, animal, or object will do. Your child can pick a character for himself, but frequently children need help in coming up with less obvious roles. You might think of three possible characters and let your child choose among them. When you offer choices, make them specific. Say he can be a *giant shark*, a *pitcher for the Chicago Cubs*, or a *rocking chair*. Don't say something vague like a *fish*, a *baseball player*, or *a piece of furniture.*

Sometimes it's good to pick a character from a book or story.

"Stuart Little, what is it really like going down a drainpipe?"

"Cinderella, why didn't you tell the prince your name at the ball?"

"Eeyore, why are you so gloomy?"

After each interview, Paul drew a picture of his character. I drew pictures, too, whenever he interviewed me. I cut a piece of typewriter paper in half. This way we each had a blank sheet of paper, 8½" x 5½". We drew on these sheets. After we drew the pictures, we pasted them into a spiral notebook. Then we wrote something about each character below the drawing. This was our scrapbook of interview personalities. From time to time we read through the book together.

One day I asked Paul, "Do you remember when you were a green alligator living deep in the jungle?" And he did remember. I felt that this marked a great step in the development of Paul's imagination.

PICTURE STORIES helped me to my first success at teaching. I was still in teachers college and was asked to take over a first-grade class. I showed up at the class feeling very nervous—and carrying under my arm a pile of pictures from magazines. Thirty children stared at me. I held up the first picture:

MATERIALS

scissors
a variety of
old and new picture magazines
such as *National Geographic,
Life, People, Photographic
World, Ranger Rick*
optional: paper
pen
tape

It was a picture of an infant anteater. But I didn't say what it was. Instead I asked one of the children, Michael, to invent a story about this unknown animal. To help Michael get started, I asked him leading questions. What is this animal? What should we call him? What has just happened to him? What will happen next? Where is he from? What does he do? What does this animal like? What scares him? Does he have enemies? How does he fight his enemies? By the time I finished asking questions, Michael was set with his story:

"This is a baby mush-mush. Mush-mushes live in the forest. This mush-mush has just finished breakfast. He eats blueberries. Now he is sleepy and wants to take a nap. His mommy is going to put him to bed and cover him with leaves. But then a huge alligator comes and tries to eat the mush-mush. Then the mush-mush runs away, and the alligator can't catch him."

An excellent story! The cute little anteater picture and my leading questions helped Michael put together a first-rate fantasy. But what really thrilled me was the enthusiastic response of the rest of the class. I found myself facing thirty hands waving, thirty voices calling "Let me try," sixty eyes gleaming.

You don't need thirty children to play this game; a single child will do. Sit down with your child and go through magazines, looking for pictures to inspire stories. Once you've invented a couple of stories, it might be a good idea to combine the game with some writing. As your child spins his yarn, you write it down. Tape the picture and the written-down story together and hang them on a wall where your child can see them.

Don't be surprised if your child wants to hear you read his own story—over and over again. He may even start reading it by himself. I know I listened to Michael read his mush-mush story at least a dozen times a day for a week.

As your child learns to write, he can do the writing himself. He should tell you the story first. Then, with your encouragement, he can write down his favorite parts:

This is a mush mush. He eats blueberries He is afraid of alligators.

A short story like this is a fine achievement for a beginning writer.

If you have a couple of children, try showing both of them the picture and seeing what different stories they invent. Each child can whisper his story to you, and you can write both down. After you write each story, share the results with the other child. It might be fun to get your children to cooperate in creating one joint story. Or it might not be fun—getting a younger and an older child to respect each other's ideas is hard to achieve. But even if they write separate stories, the game is still good for their imagination and their ability to put their imagined thoughts into words.

PART FOUR

Reading Every Day

chapter 11.

The Right Spark

Some children are uninterested in learning how to read. They may have all the necessary skills—good eye and ear perception, mastery of words, a firm knowledge of letter sounds, and a vivid imagination. But they're not motivated to learn; they need a spark to get them going, something to make them appreciate the value of reading. The philosopher Rousseau wrote his great book on education, *Emile*, about a child like this. Little Emile saw no point in learning to read. He used to receive lots of party invitations that needed to be read; but someone was always there to decipher these letters for him. One day, no one was around. An invitation arrived, but Emile couldn't figure it out by himself. The party came and went—without him. Bang! that was the spark. Emile was ready to learn how to read. Learning how was suddenly worth all the hard work involved. Emile was motivated.

What follows are some sparks, to get children feeling that reading is a valuable, irreplaceable, terrific part of life. Not every spark will fire up every child. But somewhere there's the right spark for your child, and if you experiment long enough, you'll find it. It's either that or the birch rod, and birch rods, we know, don't work at all.

Some of the following activities involve reading aloud. Others focus on making things. There's a cooking activity. There's a treasure hunt, involving a little present for your child; bribery is frequently a very good spark. The final activities suggest ways to get children interested not only in reading but in writing as well.

READING ALOUD

Most parents recognize the importance of reading aloud to very young children. But many of these same parents are surprised to hear that reading aloud is just as important for older children. They think that reading aloud to older children is unnecessary, maybe even damaging. "He won't read for himself if I read for him" is a comment I've heard all too often. Actually, the opposite is true. Reading aloud feeds a child's interest in books and increases the desire to read.

My first teaching job was as a third-grade teacher in a suburban public school. One of the things I scheduled into the day was a "book time" when I read aloud to the children. During "book time" the children were caught up in the magic of stories. Not even the best readers in the class could read as fluently as the teacher, so when I read aloud, they enjoyed the plot, the language, and the author's ideas more fully than when they read to themselves. One sign of this was the animation with which the children talked about the stories. I read novels, a chapter or two a day, and there were hot arguments about what would happen next. I read science books, and they asked questions that led to more questions that sometimes led to answers. I read biographies, and they were touched by the lives of heroic men and women; fairy tales and myths, and they thrilled to the exploits of witches and goddesses.

Sometimes I chose easy-to-read books. There's no reason why read-aloud books have to be a great intellectual challenge. Any child in the class could reread these books on his own. Sometimes I read books, especially the longer ones, that were indeed hard even for the best readers. A few children did try to reread these hard books. In doing so, they stretched their reading levels the way a swimmer builds endurance by going an extra lap. But I wouldn't have cared if these books were never reread. The benefits of reading aloud are long-term and don't depend on whether a child rereads a book or two.

The appendix "Books for Reading Aloud" lists good read-aloud choices. Librarians, bookstore clerks, other parents, and teachers can surely give more suggestions. Not every book will meet with

MATERIALS
books

cheers. Some may bore your child. Others may be good, but too difficult for your child right now. It's not hard to know if you've made a bad choice. Children are uninhibited critics. If your child gives a book a bad review, put it back on the shelf. With all the superb children's books around, there's no point in finishing a dud.

Traditionally, parents read to children at bedtime. But if bedtime is inconvenient, try other times of the day—for instance, after dinner, before homework, right after school, Saturday mornings, Sundays before lunch. You can establish a regular reading time or make it a random event. Reading aloud doesn't have to last more than ten or fifteen minutes. You may find when you start reading longer books, however, that you'll want to spend more time.

You don't need to read every day. Casual and relaxed reading three times a week—or once a week—is far better than rushed and forced reading seven times a week.

If you have more than one child, you'll want to read books that will please everybody. Unfortunately, this isn't always possible. Sometimes you'll pick a book that one child will love and another will hate; then you'll have a problem. I suggest that you finish the book, but don't insist that the child who hates it listen. Let the uninterested one draw, read on his own, or do some other quiet activity. (I wouldn't let him watch TV, since that might interfere with your reading.) With luck, this child will like the next book. If the age span between your children is great, it will be hard to find books for everyone. Separate read-aloud times might be necessary. Occasionally an older child can take your place and read aloud to a younger child.

If a child wants to hear a favorite book over and over again, that's fine. Just make sure that you regularly introduce new books, some of which may become favorites, too. You're certain to enjoy some of these books yourself. But what you may enjoy more is the cry at the end of a chapter, "Oh, don't stop now. Can't you read for five more minutes?"

COOKING

There are drawbacks to cooking with your child. It's messy, it takes longer than cooking alone, and sometimes the finished food looks peculiar. Your kitchen, your schedule, and your stomach may protest against it. But there are also benefits, especially if the child must consult a recipe in order to help you cook. When a child reads a recipe, he begins to appreciate that reading is a practical part of life.

Let's say you are making cookies. Sit down with your child and look at the recipe together. Let the child read as many words as he can: *1 cup sugar, 1 egg, mix well*, and so on. While cooking, you might make a point of referring to the recipe. Ask your child to double-check—does the recipe call for *1 cup butter* or *1 cup flour*? Just make sure this checking stays casual. You want your child to feel like a cook, not a student.

After reading the recipe, divide up the cooking tasks. Almost all recipes have some simple tasks appropriate for beginning chefs. Children make excellent pourers, stirrers, sifters, and, with supervision, measurers. You can even teach young children to use a knife to peel, slice, and chop.

Children love to cook sweet foods. But don't limit your child's cooking to desserts and snacks. I've known children to make wonderful soups, salads, casseroles, even quick breads. You might start your child's cooking career with mixes. At breakfast, let him tackle a pancake mix. At lunch, he might try a macaroni-and-cheese mix, at dinnertime experiment with a muffin mix, and later in the evening whip up cookies from a cookie mix. (But not all in one day!)

Cookbooks written especially for children do exist, but you don't really have to get one of these. Adult cookbooks have plenty of recipes easy enough for children to make. When cooking with children, I copy recipes onto a separate sheet of paper; that way I avoid gooey fingerprints all over my cookbook. In fact, it's a good idea to compile a special homemade cookbook, one that can get good and dirty. This book can include recipes copied from other books as well as those borrowed from friends, taken from pack-

MATERIALS

cookbooks
whatever else you need
for cooking
optional: notebook
pen

ages, or even original recipes invented by you or your child. The recipes can be as simple as instructions for popping popcorn or as complicated as a recipe for cherry cheesecake. All you need is a notebook filled with paper. Then start writing in the recipes. Your child will read and reread this cookbook in order to make and remake his favorite dishes.

Here are a few recipe suggestions to get your cookbook off to a delicious start.

RECIPES

Whole Wheat Muffins (makes 12 muffins)

You need:

1 egg
1 cup yogurt
1/4 cup oil
1/3 cup honey

1/2 teaspoon salt
2 tablespoons baking powder
2 cups whole wheat flour
2 muffin tins

1. Preheat oven to 350°.
2. Grease muffin tins.
3. Beat the egg.
4. Add yogurt, oil, and honey to the egg and stir.
5. Add salt, baking powder, and flour. Stir until the batter is completely mixed.
6. Pour batter into muffin tins. Each tin should be about 2/3 full.
7. Bake at 350° for 20 minutes. When done, the muffins will be golden brown, and a knife pierced into one will come out clean.

While waiting for the muffins to bake, you might try making some:

Homemade Sweet Butter

You need:
1/2 pint heavy cream
a pint jar with a tight-fitting lid

1. Pour the cream into the jar and start to shake it.
2. Keep shaking the jar; after about 15 minutes, you'll have butter shaking around in milk.
3. Drain off the milk. Wrap the butter in wax paper and refrigerate.

Making butter takes a lot of arm power. The more people there are to take turns, the better. After about ten minutes, you'll have thick whipped cream, which is very heavy. Unless your child is very strong, he won't be able to shake the jar hard enough to turn the whipped cream into butter. You must do this yourself. Once the butter begins to form, your child can take over and shake the jar until all the milk is separated from the butter.

Yogurt Shake (makes one glass)

You need:
¾ cup orange juice   1 banana
¼ cup plain yogurt   a blender

1. Pour the yogurt and orange juice into the blender.
2. Slice the banana and add it to the blender.
3. Blend at medium speed until banana is liquefied and the shake is foamy.

Homemade Peanut Butter

You need:
2 cups roasted peanuts   a blender
2 tablespoons oil   optional: salt

1. Put the nuts and oil into the blender.
2. Blend at medium speed until smooth. If you like crunchy peanut butter, stop blending before the peanut butter gets smooth.
3. Put peanut butter in a container. With a spoon or a knife, blend in salt a pinch at a time.

Fudge

You need:
1 14-ounce can of sweetened condensed milk
18 ounces semi-sweet chocolate morsels
½ teaspoon vanilla
a dash of salt
¼ cup raisins
¼ cup chopped walnuts
an 8″ x 8″ pan
butter or margarine for greasing the pan

1. Lightly butter the pan.
2. Cook milk and chocolate over low flame until chocolate melts.
3. Mix in vanilla, salt, raisins, and nuts.
4. Spread mixture in pan.
5. Refrigerate two to three hours.
6. Cut and serve.

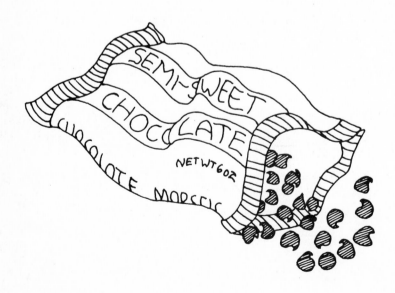

Your child comes home from school and you hand him a note:

Treasure hunt—Follow the clues in each note and you will find a treasure. The next clue is hidden under the blue chair.

Under the blue chair, he finds this note:

Congratulations, you have found the second clue. Now you must look in the rain boots in the front closet.

Inside the boots he discovers a new note:

Your next clue is hiding in a tall book on your bookshelf.

After looking on the bookshelf, and the kitchen cabinet, and under his pillow, and beneath the telephone, he finally tracks down a small, gift-wrapped box in the top drawer of your desk. Inside the box he discovers a matchbox car, a piece of dollhouse furniture, a set of jacks, or a new paperback book. The TREASURE HUNT has turned a little gift into a reading adventure.

Your child may need help reading TREASURE HUNT notes. Give all the help he needs. Eventually the notes will be easy for him to read, and he'll zoom in on the hidden treasure. Whether TREASURE HUNT clues are a reading challenge or a breeze, the game still nurtures a child's enthusiasm for reading.

My guess is that TREASURE HUNT clues will be one reading job your child asks to do over and over again.

TREASURE HUNT

MATERIALS

Index cards or notepaper

pen

tape

a surprise gift package such as a doll's dress, football cards, or a new box of crayons

LUNCH-BOX MAIL

MATERIALS

stationery

*E*ach day at lunchtime—before she ate, even before she talked to friends—Zara pulled a letter from her lunch box and read it. I watched this ritual and grew increasingly curious about her lunch-box mail. Finally I asked her about it.

"That's my lunch letter," Zara told me. "My mom writes me a letter every day. I always read it before I eat."

"May I see it?"

"Sure." She handed me the letter.

It said, "Dear Zara, Good luck on the math test today. When I get home from work, how would you like to make fudge? Yummy! Love, Mom."

I know a good idea when I see one. The next week, a father asked me what he could do to stimulate his son Billy to read. I mentioned the mail in Zara's lunch box that was making her so eager to read. If Billy received some lunch-box mail, too, it might increase his excitement about reading. Billy's father thought this sounded great. Although he knew he couldn't manage a letter every day, he started writing once or twice a week. Billy responded to the letters just as eagerly as Zara. He showed them to Carolyn and Hannah. They wanted lunch letters, too, and convinced their mothers to begin writing. More "mail" started showing up at lunch. Occasionally I stuck a note of my own into one or another lunch box.

It may have been my imagination, but I noticed a change taking place in the group. The children were more interested in reading now that it had a purpose in their lives and had become an exciting part of their day. Letters from a parent or teacher made reading exciting.

If you want to start writing lunchtime letters, here are some tips. Try to keep your language simple, but if you need to use difficult words, don't worry. Children can read surprisingly well when it is important to them. Tell your child to ask the teacher or some other good reader for help with hard words. Don't use lunch-box mail to communicate important information. If you want your child to go to a neighbor's after school, say so in person. Then use the letter as a reminder. If your child doesn't carry a lunch box, you can stick the note in a pocket or book bag. Your child should promise not to read the letter until lunchtime. Tell him you want to think about him at lunchtime, just when he is reading the letter you wrote. It's a way to feel together even when you are apart.

Lunchtime is not the only time your child will appreciate a letter. One could be waiting on the kitchen table when he returns from school. You could put a good-night note under his pillow. Leave a note for the child to read when you go out for the evening. Any time your child might miss you is a perfect time for a letter. Your note lets him know that you miss him, too. It's a fine thing for your child to associate reading with your love and concern.

REAL MAIL

MATERIALS

stationery
optional:
some drawing supplies

*H*ere are two activities that will inspire your child to become a letter writer.

Hannah not only liked receiving letters, she liked writing them, too. From the time Hannah was in kindergarten, she and her grandmother kept up a regular correspondence. Every few weeks a letter arrived from Grandmother, and every few weeks Hannah answered these letters. Grandma's letters were filled with information about Grandma and Grandpa. Grandma also asked Hannah lots of questions about school, friends, and dancing class. Every time a letter arrived, Hannah and her mother read it and talked about what Hannah wanted to write back. Then Hannah wrote the return letter. In the beginning, Hannah dictated these letters to her mother. When she got older, she copied the dictations in her own hand. Still later, she could write the letters herself. This was no problem, since tedious matters like spelling and punctuation were declared unimportant.

One reason Hannah enjoyed writing these letters was that her mother stayed by her side as she worked. Her mother expressed enthusiasm about the letters and was delighted by her daughter's growing flair for writing.

To arrange a correspondence for your child, you need to enlist an adult letter writer. The person you choose, a relative or close friend, should be someone who will understand how important regular mail will be to your child. Pick a person who will be supportive, not critical, of your child's writing.

If setting up a regular correspondence is impractical, then you and your child can limit letters to special occasions. Instead of going out and buying valentines, birthday cards, holiday greetings, or party invitations, develop a family tradition of making your own. If your child is sending a birthday message, help him think about what makes a birthday important. What birthday wish does he want to send? What is the best thing about a birthday? With your encouragement, he will write more than a plain "Happy Birthday." Your child may enjoy illustrating these letters with crayons, colored pencils, or colored markers.

FAMILY CALENDAR

*T*he complaint I hear most from parents is, "My child never tells me what goes on in school. When I ask about the day, all I hear is, 'Oh, nothing much happened.'" A FAMILY CALENDAR is a way to get a child talking about his or her day. And it's an opportunity to make reading and writing part of your family's daily life.

A FAMILY CALENDAR is a cross between an engagement book and a diary. The calendar keeps track of your family's plans for the week and, at the same time, records how you all feel about the things you do. A calendar has several benefits for you and your children. You will find out about your children's day; they'll find out about your day; they'll be learning to express themselves; and all this will take place around a reading-and-writing activity.

Calendars are easy to make. First design a few blank sheets of paper as calendar pages.

Use colored felt-tip markers to make them look bright. Put these sheets in a plastic folder. On the first sheet, write the date of the current week, and you're ready to start.

Sunday night is a good time to begin. Gather as many of your family as you can and think about the upcoming week. Does anyone have special plans? Is there something to look forward to, this coming week, or something to be worried about? It may turn out that you are having lunch with an old friend on Wednesday; your daughter Katrina is concerned about her dental appointment on Tuesday; your son Robert is excited about Sylvia's birthday party on Friday. Talk about these events for a few minutes. Where will you be eating lunch? Why is it exciting to see this old friend? What do you think you'll talk about? Why is Katrina worried about going to the dentist? What's the worst that can happen at the dentist's? What does it feel like to get a cavity filled? Why is Robert looking forward to the birthday party? What games is he hoping to play? What present does he want to buy for his friend? Then bring the discussion to a close and fill in the calendar.

On Wednesday evening, take out the calendar and talk about the week so far. Mom's lunch was fun. Her friend had interesting

MATERIALS
blank paper
felt-tip markers
pen
plastic folder

WEEK OF						
SUN.	MON.	TUE.	WED.	THUR.	FRI.	SAT.

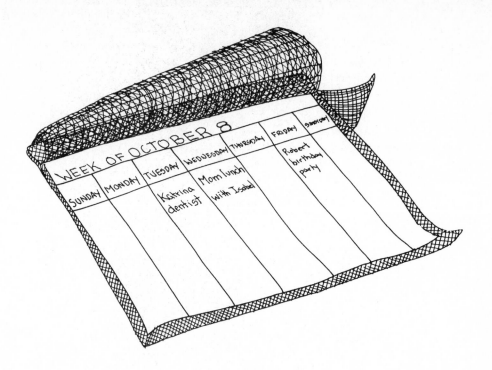

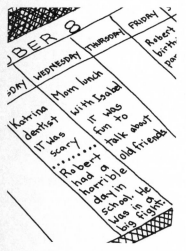

news and gossip about people Mom hadn't seen in a long time. Katrina's dental appointment was truly horrible and terrifying. Thank goodness Katrina didn't have any cavities and there was nothing for the dentist to do. Robert had a bad day in school on Tuesday. He'd been in a fight with three other boys, and the teacher punished only Robert. It was the worst day in school ever. Mom has decided that Saturday is going to be shoe-buying day. As you talk, update the calendar.

From time to time, as the calendar book fills up, you might enjoy reading old pages and sharing memories. There was that time Robert invited Adam to sleep over, and they stayed up until midnight laughing and talking—boy, was Mom angry! You can save the calendar, by the way, and take it out twenty years later. Ah, you'll say; this is when Robert and Katrina were learning to read.

Nick was a second-grader with a special passion. It didn't take long to discover what it was. First clue, a Yankee baseball cap. Second clue, a Yankee baseball jacket. Third clue, the smile on his face when I said, "I bet you like baseball." Naturally Nick had a shoebox full of baseball cards. Here was a way to stimulate his interest in reading. We'd make a baseball card scrapbook that he could read.

I bought an inexpensive scrapbook at the 5 & 10, wrapped it as a gift, and presented it to Nick. We selected some of his favorite cards and taped them into the book. Then Nick wrote a comment about each player directly below the card. At first I did the actual writing, according to what he told me. Later I wrote his comments on a sheet of paper, and he copied them into the scrapbook. Ultimately, he did everything himself.

MATERIALS

scrapbook
pen
paper
glue or transparent tape
scissors
(additional materials will depend on your child's choice of a scrapbook collection)

This is Johnny Bench. He started in the major leagues in 1967. In 1982 he became the 52nd player in history to get 1,300 runs batted in.

This is John Mayberry. He plays first base for the Yankees. He weighs 220 pounds.

Scrapbooks with recorded comments can be assembled around almost any interest your child has. You can start the book with a few pages, then enlarge it as time goes on. Consider a scrapbook of family trips, using photographs and postcards. Each family member can write a comment about the picture. You may find it easier to write these comments on a separate sheet of paper and then tape the comment sheet into the scrapbook.

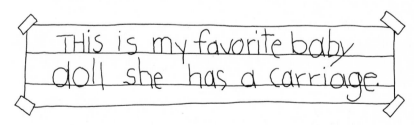

Mom: I remember how beautiful it was on top of the mountain. I thought I could see forever.

Dad: We saw the most amazing flowers on the mountain top.

Julie: The peanut butter sandwich I ate on the mountian was good.

If your child has a doll collection, you can make a doll scrapbook. Take snapshots of the dolls in all their various outfits, put the snapshots in the scrapbook, and add brief comments.

THIS is my favorite baby doll she has a carriage.

You can make a pet scrapbook in the same way. Photograph your dog, cat, guinea pig, gerbil, or iguana at their most dog-, cat-, guinea-pig-, gerbil-, or iguana-like moments. Put the photographs in the scrapbook and your child can write the captions.

This is my cat Pooh. He is eating. He loves to eat. He loves liver. I hate liver.

You can add other animals to this scrapbook. You could turn it into a collection of animals from around the world. Do this by cutting pictures out of nature magazines like *National Geographic*, *Natural History*, or *Ranger Rick.*

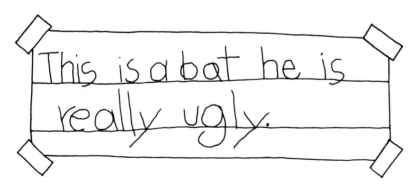

This is a bat he is really ugly.

If your child is a car enthusiast, make a car collection. Get automotive magazines, cut out pictures of favorite cars, and fill your scrapbook. If he is a nature buff, build a collection of dried leaves and flowers. If he loves movies and TV, make a scrapbook with photographs taken from fan magazines.

It is an excellent thing if your child writes most of the captions for himself. If writing is beyond him, however, and you do it instead, the activity still has value. Your child will be enthusiastic about his scrapbook in large part because you and he work on it together. Hunting through magazines, discovering a baby koala picture, deciding on captions, cutting, pasting, writing in turns, and finally reading the book together—all this makes SCRAP-BOOK COLLECTIONS a joy.

LITERARY LION

*E*ven the greatest writers begin their careers humbly. Edmund Wilson began as a little boy dictating stories to his aunt. She wrote the stories down and bound them into small books. These little books encouraged young Edmund's interest in writing and, at the same time, provided him with books he was delighted to read—books written by himself.

You can make a collection of your own child's little books, thought up by him and written down by you. When a child is ready, suggest that he do the writing himself. It helps if you are absolutely unconcerned about the niceties of spelling and punctuation. If a child doesn't want to write, don't force him. I remember one fifth-grader who hated writing. His stories were always as short as he could make them. One day I agreed to write for him. He dictated a thirty-page story—a major breakthrough. So there are advantages to taking dictation even after a child can write for himself.

Begin by helping your child to think up a story idea. The child's mind may already be filled with possibilities, but just in case he has trouble thinking of subjects, here are some titles for inspiration:

> The Bank Robbery
> The Adventure in a Flying Balloon
> The Worst Nightmare
> The Day I Played Baseball with the Yankees
> Life of a Witch's Cat
> The Car Race
> The UFO
> If I Were My Mother

These are make-believe stories. True-life experiences make wonderful stories, too. Any event in a child's life can become a story: a baseball game in the park, a museum trip to see dinosaur bones, getting a pet kitten. If, after selecting a title, a child finds it hard to get the story off the ground, help out by asking questions. How

MATERIALS

paper
pencil or pen
**crayons, colored pencils,
or colored markers**
folders
stapler

did you get the kitten? Why did you pick that kitten? What are some funny things the kitten does? What is the best thing about having a kitten? I've found these questions and a little discussion generate stories, at least short ones, from even the most hesitant child. As soon as your child starts talking, you start writing. Write down everything he says, mistakes and all. When you read the story back to your child, if he wants to change anything, that's OK.

Here is what the book will look like when it is finished: several pages of writing with illustrations, bound with staples or enclosed in a folder. A book can consist of a single story, a story made up of chapters, or several different stories bound together. You'll want to write the stories so that they can easily be bound into an attractive book. For this reason, leave a margin on the left-hand side and a space on each page for your child's illustrations. It's best to use only one side of each sheet of paper. When the story is written, your child can make a title page that serves as the book cover.

The easiest way to bind the book is to run staples along the margin—presto, a book. A slightly more formal book can be made by using a folder. I like to use the colored plastic folders with the color-coordinated ribs. By making every book a different color, your child can have a rainbow-colored book collection. To make the book childproof, secure the pages with a few staples under the rib. One nice aspect of the plastic folder is that the title page, with its illustration, shows through the tinted plastic.

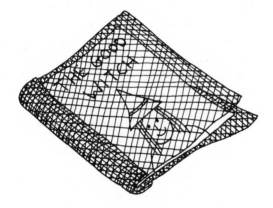

There it is, your child's own, original book—an accomplishment to be proud of. You can foster the feeling of pride by the care and respect you show for these books. You might devote part of a bookshelf to your child's storybooks, or keep the books on a special table. Try reading your child's book aloud at bedtime, just as you read any other good author. Suggest that he share his stories with other people. He can read them to baby-sitters, grandparents, brothers, sisters, or teachers. Favorite stories can be photocopied and given as gifts. You can mail books to friends and relatives living out of town. In effect, you'll be publishing a first edition of your child's selected stories.

READING
TOGETHER

What about when your child knows how to read? Here's a way to encourage him or her to take pleasure in reading. Arrange things so that you and your child read together side by side, each with his own book or magazine. Pick a convenient time for regular reading; it might be every day or a couple of times a week. The important thing is to set up a pattern and stick to it. Regular routines tend to become habits, and you want reading to be a habit that's hard for your child to break. Once you make it clear that six o'clock Friday evenings is reading time, there will be less hullabaloo when six comes. The child will think: reading time is reading time; why fight it? Once the routine is established, you can be more flexible. Then, if necessary, reading time can be postponed—"I'm sorry, dear, we won't be able to read together today. We'll make up for it Sunday."

Some days you may want to spend only ten minutes reading. Other days it will feel right to spend fifteen or twenty minutes, or even half an hour. In general, you should each read your own books, but don't make this a rigid rule. Some days, read aloud to your child from his book. Other days, let him read to you. On occasion, talk about the books you've each been reading.

You'll want to make sure your child has a supply of good books to read. A good book is exciting; a bad book is a bore. Check the appendix of "Easy Reading Books" for some of my favorites. Ask librarians, teachers, friends, or bookstore clerks to suggest especially good books. Another appendix lists children's magazines. Children, like adults, love to get their own magazines in the mail.

It is possible that your child will resist sitting down with you to read. But stay with the effort for at least a week or two. Here are some tricks to motivate enthusiasm. Try reading the beginning of the book aloud. When the plot is established and the child's interest in the story is assured, stop reading. To find out what happens next, he'll have to read on by himself. A second trick is to browse through the book together, stopping now and again to discuss the illustrations. Using illustrations as clues, make guesses about the story. "I wonder why that cat has such a funny expression. I bet he's up to no good." When your child's interest in the story is aroused, hand him the book and let him read. Another technique is to buy your child a brand-new book. Wrap the book as a special gift. Excitement over the gift may motivate him to read the book. Or give your child a book that was one of your childhood favorites. Exclaim over how special the book was to you, how much you loved the story, how you read it many times. This should make him curious to try the book for himself. If all else fails, try bribery. Promise a game of checkers or a helping hand with chores when reading time is over.

If a child still resists reading, then stop for the time being. You can always try again in a month, or next fall. Just make sure that reading doesn't become a punishment. If you and your child start fighting over reading, the child will learn to hate books and reading, too—which would be terrible. Easy does it, then.

By the way, it's excellent to let your child see you reading. Children imitate their parents. If sitting with a book or magazine seems an adult thing to do in your home, your child may eventually want to be seen with a book or magazine, too. Good—extremely good.

Appendices

A LIST OF
IMPORTANT WORDS

In judging under which category to list a word, I have taken into consideration not only the intrinsic difficulty of the word, but also the frequency with which it appears in children's literature. That's why *many*, a word used with great frequency, is in the easy category, while *best*, a word that is just as easy to read but appears less frequently, is in the toughie category.

Easy Words

a	come	her	no	tell
all	day	here	not	that
am	did	him	now	the
an	do	house	of	them
and	dog	how	old	then
are	down	I	on	they
as	eat	if	one	this
ask	find	in	or	three
at	for	into	out	to
ate	funny	is	play	too
away	get	it	put	top
be	girl	jump	ran	two
big	give	let	red	up
black	go	like	ride	us
blue	going	look	run	was
boy	good	made	sad	we
brown	got	make	said	well
but	had	man	saw	will
by	has	many	say	with
call	hat	me	see	woman
came	have	mouse	she	work
can	he	must	sit	yellow
car	help	my	so	yes
cat	hen	new	stop	you

Intermediate Words

after
again
airplane
any
apple
baby
ball
barn
bear
bed
bell
bird
birthday
boat
book
box
bus
cake
call
can't
cap
chair
city
climb
coat
cold
corn
cow
cry
cut

dark
doll
door
drive
duck
easy
egg
elephant
end
every
eve
fall
far
farm
fast
fat
father
feet
fire
first
fish
five
floor
fly
four
fox
friend
frog
from
gave

goes
gone
green
happy
hello
hide
horse
hot
just
keep
king
kitten
know
last
late
laugh
leg
light
lion
little
live
lost
may
milk
mother
Mr.
Mrs.
name
next
night

once
open
orange
other
our
over
people
pick
pig
please
pretty
pull
puppy
queen
rabbit
read
right
room
shop
sing
sleep
some
something
soon
start
store
street
sun
table
take

talk
ten
thank
there
thing
think
time
took
top
toy
tree
try
under
use
very
walk
want
wash
way
went
were
what
when
where
white
who
why
your
zoo

Toughie Words

about	country	high	own	their
across	does	hill	paper	these
always	done	hold	party	those
animal	don't	hurt	picture	thought
another	draw	kind	pony	through
around	drink	learn	rain	today
back	each	left	ring	together
basket	eight	letter	road	train
beautiful	end	long	round	until
because	enough	lunch	school	upon
been	farmer	maybe	self	voice
before	field	might	seven	wagon
began	flower	mind	shall	wait
behind	found	money	sheep	warm
best	full	monkey	shoe	watch
better	garden	more	should	water
both	glad	morning	show	which
bread	goat	move	sister	window
bring	grandfather	much	six	wish
brother	grandmother	myself	small	won't
buy	grass	near	squirrel	wood
carry	great	never	stay	would
change	grow	nest	stick	write
chicken	happen	nose	sure	yard
children	hand	nothing	surprise	year
clean	head	only	teacher	yet

A LIST OF IMPORTANT SOUNDS

Level One

b, c (as in *cat* and *cent*), d, f, g (as in *gem* and *good*), h, j, k, l, m, n, p, q, r, s, t, v, w, x (as in *ax* and *xylophone*), y (as in *yarn*), z

Level Two

All of Level One plus:
The long and short vowel sounds, which are:
a as in *ate* and *at*
e as in *eat* and *egg*
i as in *ice* and *ink*
o as in *oat* and *otter*
u as in *use* and *us*
Also in Level Two are:
y (as in *my* and *happy*)
ar (as in *car*), er (as in *her*), ir (as in *bird*), or (as in *or*),
ur (as in *turn*)

Level Three

All of Levels One and Two plus:
bl, br, cl, cr, dr, fl, fr, gl, gr, pl, pr, sc, sk, sl, sm, sn, sp, st, sw, tr, tw, ch, th, sh, wh

Level Four

All of Levels One, Two, and Three plus:
sch, scr, shr, spl, spr, squ, str, thr, nd, nk, ng, nt, ft, ai, al, ay, oa, ea, ee, oe, ue

Level Five

All of Levels One, Two, Three, and Four plus:
au, aw, ew, oi, ou (as in *out* and *trouble*) ow (as in *cow* and *blow*), oo (as in *boot* and *foot*)

BOOKS FOR READING ALOUD

Here is a list of books that you may enjoy reading to your child. A good read-aloud book must have a story that is simple enough for a child to follow easily. It must be intelligent enough to keep an adult's interest. It must be well written; a badly written book sounds even worse when read aloud. Some of these books may be too complicated or lengthy for your child to enjoy right now, in which case, wait and try again next year. There's only one sure-fire way to know if a book is right for your child—read one or two chapters and see what the reaction is. If, after a chapter or two, your child vetoes the book, pick a different one.

I've arranged the books in five categories (fiction, non-fiction, poetry, fairy tales, and activity books), and whenever possible I've listed the books in order of difficulty, beginning with the easiest. But with many of these books, there's no saying which is easy and which is hard, so don't take that aspect of the list too seriously.

Fiction

The Story of Babar by Jean de Brunhoff
Bartholomew and the Oobleck by Dr. Seuss
Winnie-the-Pooh by A. A. Milne
The House at Pooh Corner by A. A. Milne
My Father's Dragon by Ruth Stiles Gannett
Just So Stories by Rudyard Kipling
Mrs. Piggle-Wiggle (or any of the other books in the Mrs. Piggle-Wiggle series) by Betty MacDonald
The Boxcar Children by Gertrude Chandler Warner
Stuart Little by E. B. White
Charlotte's Web by E. B. White
Superfudge by Judy Blume
Freckle Juice by Judy Blume
Ramona the Pest by Beverly Cleary

Mr. Popper's Penguins by Richard and Florence Atwater
The Town Cats and Other Tales by Lloyd Alexander
Half Magic by Edward Eager
The Wizard of Oz by L. Frank Baum
Pippi Longstocking by Astrid Lindgren
The Borrowers by Mary Norton
The Animal Family by Randall Jarrell
The Enormous Egg by Oliver Butterworth
Homer Price by Robert McCloskey
The Real Thief by William Steig
Sounder by William Armstrong
The Chronicles of Narnia by C. S. Lewis
How to Eat Fried Worms by Thomas Rockwell
Tuck Everlasting by Natalie Babbitt

Non-Fiction

Why Don't You Get a Horse, Sam Adams? by Jean Fritz
And Then What Happened, Paul Revere? by Jean Fritz
Meet Martin Luther King by James T. DeKay
Wanted Dead or Alive: The True Story of Harriet Tubman by Ann McGovern
If You Lived in Colonial Times by Ann McGovern
Sadako and the Thousand Paper Cranes by Eleanor Coerr
Baseball Players Do Amazing Things by Mel Cebulash
How to Be a Nature Detective by Millicent Selsam
Animals Do the Strangest Things by Leonora and Arthur Hornblow

Poetry

When We Were Very Young by A. A. Milne
Now We Are Six by A. A. Milne
Spin a Soft Black Song by Nikki Giovanni
Oh What Nonsense! edited by William Cole
A Light in the Attic by Shel Silverstein
Where the Sidewalk Ends by Shel Silverstein

The Random House Book of Poetry for Children selected by Jack
   Prelutsky
The Moment of Wonder edited by Richard Lewis
Miracles by Richard Lewis
Piping Down the Valleys Wild edited by Nancy Larrick

Fairy and Folk Tales

Fairy Tales by E. E. Cummings
Peach Boy and Other Stories by Florence Sakade
Clever Gretchen and Other Forgotten Folktales by Alison Lurie
The Classic Fairy Tales edited by Iona and Peter Opie
Black Folk Tales by Julius Lester
Tatterhood and Other Tales edited by Ethel Johnston
Jack Tales by Richard Chase
Zlateh the Goat and Other Stories by I. B. Singer
The Juniper Tree translated by Lore Segal and Randall Jarrell from
   Grimm's tales
D'Aulaire's Book of Greek Myths by Ingri and Edgar D'Aulaire
American Folk Tales by Adrien Stoutenburg
The Happy Prince and Other Stories by Oscar Wilde
Pantheon Fairy Tale and Folklore Library, especially:
   Russian Fairy Tales by Aleksandr Afanas'ev
   The Complete Grimm's Fairy Tales
   Italian Folktales by Italo Calvino
   Chinese Fairy Tales and Fantasies edited by Moss Roberts

Activity Books

(There aren't many activity books that can be read aloud with
pleasure. Here are a few of the best.)
Make-Believe Empire: A How-To Book by Paul Berman
The Brown Paper School Series, especially:
   My Backyard History Book by David Weitzman
   The I Hate Mathematics! Book by Marilyn Burns
   Good for Me! by Marilyn Burns

206

EASY READING BOOKS

Easy reading books are for beginning readers to read by themselves or with your help. First-graders almost always need help with these books, and second- and third-graders often do, too. When your child has trouble reading a word, it's better not to tell him to sound it out; just read it for him. That way the flow of the story isn't interrupted for a lesson in letter sounds.

I've arranged the following book list in order of difficulty, from easy to less easy. Often several easy reading books are written as a series, and in these cases I've given the name of the series rather than list each book separately.

Little Bear books by Else Minarik
Last One Home Is a Green Pig by Edith Thacher Hurd
Are You My Mother? by P. D. Eastman
The Cat in the Hat books by Dr. Seuss
Clifford the Big Red Dog books by Norman Bridwell
Cowboy Andy by Edna Walker Chandler
Kick, Pass, and Run by Leonard Kessler
Sam and the Firefly by P. D. Eastman
Sammy the Seal by Syd Hoff
Danny and the Dinosaur by Syd Hoff
Mine's the Best by Crosby Bonsall
Fox and His Friends by Edward Marshall
Walking Shoes by Anne Rockwell
The Secret Three by Mildred Myrick
Meet M and M by Pat Ross
George and Martha books by James Marshall
Frog and Toad books by Arnold Lobel
Three by the Sea by Edward Marshall
Arthur books by Lillian Hoban
Billy and Blaze books by C. W. Anderson
The Case of the Hungry Stranger and other *Case of . . .* books
   by Crosby Bonsall

Nate the Great books by Marjorie Weinman Sharmat
Dinosaur Time by Peggy Parrish
No More Monsters for Me! by Peggy Parrish
No Fighting, No Biting by Else Minarik
Sleeping Ugly by Jane Yolen
Wiley and the Hairy Man by Molly Garrett Bung
Sam, the Minuteman by Nathaniel Benchley
A Ghost Named Fred by Nathaniel Benchley
Amelia Bedelia books by Peggy Parrish

CHILDREN'S MAGAZINES

Cobblestone, 28 Main Street, Peterborough, N.H. 03458 (a history magazine)
Cricket, Box 100, La Salle, Ill. 61301 (a literary magazine)
Highlights for Children, 2300 West Fifth Avenue, P.O. Box 269, Columbus, Ohio 43216
National Geographic World, National Geographic Society, Washington, D.C. 20036
Ranger Rick's Nature Magazine, National Wildlife Federation, 1412 16th Street, N.W., Washington, D.C. 20036
Stone Soup, P.O. Box 83, Santa Cruz, Cal. 95063 (stories written by children)

A NOTE TO TEACHERS

Games for Reading can be used perfectly well in the classroom. Many of the games are adaptable for work with small groups. A game like WORD BINGO simply requires extra bingo boards. DO THIS, DO THAT can be played in a group if children take turns following instructions. OOPS can be transformed into a team game; the first team to go "oops" loses. As you read the book, you'll see ways to modify other games as well.

A few games can be played with an entire class. CIRCLE STORY, GO-TOGETHERS, and CRAZY ANSWERS are examples. If your class is accustomed to taking turns, games like WHERE'S THE SOUND?, STORY WORDS, or PROBLEMS AND SOLUTIONS can also be played. Along about February, when it's hard to come up with new ways to teach vocabulary words or train auditory discrimination, these games may rekindle classroom energy.

You can also choose games for a teacher's aide or parent volunteer or you yourself to play with individual children. Read the instructions for a game like PURPLE PENGUINS or SEE IT—NAME IT and play it first with Johnny, then Kara, then Sam.

You might encourage parents to play games at home; simply pick out some games for them that suit their children's needs. If a child's visual memory is weak, send home instructions for SET THE TABLE or PICTURE MEMORY. If a reading group is learning vowel sounds, you might propose SOUND TOSS or RABBIT SOUNDS for playing at home. By including parents in this way, you can make your job a bit easier, make parents partners in their children's education, and give children individual help in reading.

The activities in *Games for Reading* cover all the basic reading skills. Theories about teaching reading vary quite a bit. Some educators believe that beginning readers should be taught phonics exclusively; others believe that phonics should never be taught. Some educators use language-experience activities exclusively; others will only work with a controlled vocabulary. My own view is eclectic. Experience has led me to believe that each of the major approaches to teaching reading has merit, and that ideally all the methods should be used together. *Games for Reading* follows this eclectic principle and encourages the broadest possible range of reading skills.

To assist you, as a teacher, in using these activities as part of your curriculum, I have provided below a chapter-by-chapter description of the specific skills addressed by this book. It will help you to identify quickly which parts of the book meet the goals you've set for your class. In organizing it, I have relied on the excellent system of classifying auditory and visual skills developed in Eleanor Semel's *The Semel Auditory Processing Program* and Marianne Frostig's *The Developmental Program In Visual Perception*.

Part One: Games for Learning Words

Chapter One: Words Everywhere is a collection of games that teach vocabulary words. These games are consistent with the language-experience approach to reading.

Chapter Two: Games for the Eye trains visual perception. Here is a list of the skills addressed:
visual memory (remembering what is seen)
visual discrimination (distinguishing similar shapes)
figure-ground relationship (focusing on specific visual stimuli)
spatial relationships (identifying the relative positions of objects in space)
visual constancy (recognizing shapes regardless of size or position)
directionality (telling left from right and top from bottom)
visual sequencing (perceiving visual stimuli in proper order)
visual-motor coordination (recording what you see)
visualization (forming a mental picture of things you see)
Training in these visual skills is especially important for children learning to read by the look-and-say method.

Chapter Three: Word Games is made up of games that offer drill on basic sight vocabulary. Many of these games refer to the appendix "A List of Important Words," which includes the complete Dolch list of 220 basic sight words as well as the Dolch list of 96 important nouns. The "List" also includes words gathered from pre-primer through third-grade basal readers.

Chapter Three includes, in addition, games to help children go from word-by-word reading to reading words in groups or phrases.

Part Two: Games for Learning Sounds

Chapter Four: Games for the Ear gives children practice in auditory perception. The skills children will exercise in these games include:

auditory memory (remembering what is heard)

auditory synthesis (forming a word from individual sounds)

auditory analysis (identifying sounds within a word)

auditory discrimination (hearing the differences between sounds)

sequencing (remembering the order of isolated sounds)

integration (linking audition to other modalities—for example, visual perception and motor coordination)

attentiveness (being aware of specific sounds)

reauditorization (silently repeating a sound or a word)

auditory feedback (repeating a series of sounds in order)

These auditory skills are necessary for successful work in phonics.

Chapter Five: Letter Sounds develops children's phonetic analysis. The games also form a strong link between perceiving sounds and establishing the sound/letter relationship.

Chapter Six: Super Sounds Games offers a more complete program of phonetic analysis than Chapter Five. The games in this chapter make use of the appendix "A List of Important Sounds." By playing these games, children learn consonant sounds, long vowels, short vowels, vowels modified by *r*, *w*, and *l*, hard and soft sounds for *c* and *g*, two-letter consonant blends, three-letter consonant blends, blend endings, digraphs, vowel combinations, and diphthongs.

Chapter Seven: Making Words teaches word-attack skills. In some of these games, children must integrate phonetic components into words. In others, children must rely on phonetic analysis to decode words.

Part Three: Games for Understanding

Chapter Eight: What Does That Mean? develops oral vocabulary. Having a good vocabulary consists of learning the meaning of a wide range of words, achieving good verbal recall, being able to classify and categorize words, possessing knowledge of synonyms and antonyms, and developing the ability to use vocabulary in grammatically correct ways.

Chapter Nine: Making Sense covers various aspects of reading comprehension. These include grasping the main idea of a story, paying attention to story sequence, using context clues, being able to predict outcomes, recalling details, and drawing logical conclusions.

Chapter Ten: Imagination reinforces all the skills in Chapter Nine. It also helps children to learn to use language in a sustained flow, to describe events, and to develop imaginative capacity, facility in character analysis, and a sense of story structure.

Part Four: Reading Every Day

Chapter Eleven: The Right Spark has an especially broad and significant orientation. The games in previous chapters give children skills necessary in reading. But these skills are only a means to an end. Being able to sound out words or recall basic vocabulary is not the goal; the goal is for children to become interested and independent readers. The games in *The Right Spark* specifically address that goal. Many of the ideas in this chapter are consistent with a language-experience teaching technique.

ABOUT THE AUTHOR

Peggy Kaye has a master's degree from Teachers College, Columbia University. She has taught at the Evans Park Elementary School in upstate New York and at the Ethical Culture School and Little Star of Broome in New York City, and was both classroom teacher and reading specialist at the Learning Community, an alternative elementary school in New York City.